Journal of Prisoners on Prisons

I0039765

... allowing our experiences and analysis to be added to the forum that will constitute public opinion could help halt the disastrous trend toward building more fortresses of fear which will become in the 21ˢᵗ century this generation's monuments to failure.

Jo-Ann Mayhew (1988)

Volume 19(1)
2010

JOURNAL OF PRISONERS ON PRISONS

EDITORIAL STAFF:

Editor-in-Chief:	Bob Gaucher	Issue Editor:	Bell Gale Chevigny
Associate Editors:	Susan Nagelsen	Prisoners' Struggles Editor:	Kevin Walby
	Charles Huckelbury	Book Review Editor:	Patrick Derby
Managing Editors:	Justin Piché	Typesetter:	Brad Horning
	Mike Larsen		

EDITORIAL BOARD:

Ramona Brockett	Liz Elliott	Michael Lenza	Stephen Richards
Panagiota Chrisovergis	Sara Falconer	Tara Lyons	Viviane Saleh-Hanna
Elizabeth Comack	Sylvie Frigon	MaDonna Maidment	Judah Schept
Howard Davidson	Bob Gaucher	Joane Martel	Renita Seabrook
Claire Delisle	Kristen Gilchrist	Erin McCuaig	Rashad Shabazz
Patrick Derby	Anne-Marie Grondin	Dawn Moore	Lisa Smith
Leah DeVellis	Kelly Hannah-Moffatt	Melissa Munn	Dale Spencer
Giselle Dias	Stacey Hannem	Peter Murphy	Brian Chad Starks
Daniel Dos Santos	Charles Hucklebury	Susan Nagelsen	Karen Emily Suurtamm
Aaron Doyle	Jennifer Kilty	Justin Piché	Kevin Walby
	Mike Larsen	Stephen Reid	Matt Yeager

The *Journal of Prisoners on Prisons* is published twice a year. Its purpose is to encourage research on a wide range of issues related to crime, justice, and punishment by prisoners and former prisoners. Donations to the *JPP* are gratefully received.

SUBMISSIONS:

Prisoners and former prisoners are encouraged to submit original papers, collaborative essays, discussions transcribed from tape, book reviews, and photo or graphic essays that have not been published elsewhere. The *Journal* does not usually publish fiction or poetry. The *Journal* will publish articles in either French or English. Articles should be no longer than 20 pages typed and double-spaced or legibly handwritten. Electronic submissions are gratefully received. Writers may elect to write anonymously or under a pseudonym. For references cited in an article, the writer should attempt to provide the necessary bibliographic information. Refer to the references cited in this issue for examples. Submissions are reviewed by members of the Editorial Board. Selected articles are corrected for composition and returned to the authors for their approval before publication. Papers not selected are returned with editor's comments. Revised papers may be resubmitted. Please submit biographical and contact information, to be published alongside articles unless otherwise indicated.

SUBSCRIPTIONS, SUBMISSIONS, AND ALL OTHER CORRESPONDENCE:

Journal of Prisoners on Prisons
c/o University of Ottawa Press
542 King Edward Avenue
Ottawa, Ontario, Canada K1N 6N5

e-mail: jpp@uottawa.ca
website: www.jpp.org

SUBSCRIPTIONS:	One Year	Two Years	Three Years
Prisoners	$11.00	$20.00	$30.00
Individuals	$22.00	$38.00	$50.00
Prison Libraries & Schools, Libraries & Institutions	$35.00	$65.00	$95.00

Canadian subscriptions payable in Canadian dollars. Canadian orders include GST. Subscriptions outside Canada payable in U.S. or Canadian dollars. Add four dollars for postage.

INDIVIDUAL COPIES AND BACK ISSUES:

$14 each (Canadian $ in Canada – U.S. $ outside of Canada) available from University of Toronto Press Distribution.

University of Toronto Press Inc.
5201 Dufferin Street
Toronto, Ontario M3H 5T8

phone: 1-800-565-9523
fax: 1-800-221-9985
e-mail: utpbooks@utpress.utoronto.ca
website: www.utpress.utoronto.ca/utp_D1/home.htm

Co-published by the *Journal of Prisoners on Prisons and* the University of Ottawa Press.

ISSN 0838-164X
ISBN 978-0-7766-0936-2

In This Issue

NOTE FROM THE MANAGING EDITORS

The Prisoners' Pen at the Crossroads
Mike Larsen and Justin Piché

This special issue of the *Journal of Prisoners on Prisons* (JPP) celebrates the PEN American Center's Prison Writing Program. Issue editor Bell Gale Chevigny – a dedicated, long-time advocate for and facilitator of prison writing – has compiled a collection of articles that includes past PEN American Center prize-winning narratives and new contributions solicited for this edition of the *JPP*.

Continuing with the themes discussed in Volume 18(1&2), this issue again focuses on the experiences and socio-politics of incarceration in the United States as revealed through the written works of prison writers as well as the accounts of educators, facilitators, and documentary filmmakers who work to foster expression that transcends institutional barriers. This collection is intended to offer a glimpse into the largest penal system in the "free world", one the Conservative Administration in Canada seems intent on mimicking despite the overwhelming evidence that the "race to incarcerate" has had a negligible impact on 'crime', with fiscal and human costs that have shown to not be worth the price of purchase (see Mauer, 1999; Mauer and Chesney-Lind, 2002).

As Susan Nagelsen, Associate Editor of the *JPP*, notes in her *Response*, this issue represents a welcome collaboration between groups that share a mandate for fostering and providing a vehicle for writing as resistance. The importance of prison writing and an appreciation for the venues that make it possible have been subjects of discussion and analysis in these pages since the inception of the *JPP*, and this issue joins a number of previous editions that have made writing, expression, and the penal press their focus.[1]

While this volume focuses on the United States, the articles speak to "carceral universals" (Gaucher, 2008, p. 2) that transcend history and geography. Prisoners the world over will hear echoes of their own experiences in Michael Rothwell's discussion of suicide and self-harm, and William Steed Kelley's account of endemic violence. Christopher J. Best's contribution is in many ways particular to the context of Texas Death Row, but his effort to make sense of institutionalized murder resonates with the literature on prisons as spaces epitomizing the biopolitics of disposability (see Bauman 2004; Byrd 1995; Giroux 2009). And anyone, anywhere, who has ever attempted to work with, survive, or resist the penal system will identify with Patrica Prewitt's excellent account of the contradictory and Kafkaesque prison bureaucracy. This bureaucracy serves to discipline and micro-regulate life on the inside, while simultaneously managing or prohibiting 'outsider' access to the prison. As noted by filmmaker Susanne Mason (this issue, p. 84), "the walls work both ways".

Thankfully, efforts to transcend and overcome the walls also work both ways, and the written word is a powerful vehicle for this. Prison writing is often a lifeline – a means to resist the dehumanizing and totalizing experience of incarceration through expression and creativity. As Bell Chevigny (1999, p. xxiv) observes in her anthology *Doing Time*, "many prisoners write as if their lives depend on it. Quite often they do". Writing is also a means to counter-inscribe the prison-industrial complex by deconstructing its core narratives and advancing alternative discourses borne of experience (Gaucher, 2002, p. 21). Further, we would argue that the writings of prisoners on prisons contribute to an evolving institutional memory that links persons, places and policies. In other words, it is possible to read the folly of next year's carceral expansion agenda in the decade-old account of a prisoner who has lived through a similar experience.

We, in Canada and in the United States, find ourselves at a crossroads. Faced with the reality that the construction and operation of carceral institutions diverts important funds from vital services such as education and health care, particularly in a time of economic crisis, many American States are considering measures to sharply reduce their reliance on imprisonment as a panacea to social problems. At the same time, the Canadian federal government is conducting a needs assessment to decide whether or not to construct new penitentiaries for men at a rate not seen since the 1960s, 1970s and 1980s (see Jackson and Stewart, 2009). At this stage of the carceral game, one where lives and futures are at stake, the *JPP* seeks to contribute to this debate through the prisoners' pen.

We were excited when Bell approached us with the idea for this issue, and we hope that you will find it as engaging as we do.

ENDNOTES

[1]   See, for example, Bob Gaucher's *Response* in the first issue of the *JPP*, "The Prisoner as Ethnographer", as well as *JPP* Volume 2(1) (1989), on "The Penal Press and

Selected Articles", Volume 10(1&2) on "Prison Writing and Prison Writers", and the *JPP* Anthology "Writing as Resistance" (2002). Prison writing is, of course, a core underlying theme in every issue of the *JPP*, and an issue at the heart of our mandate as a journal.

REFERENCES

Bauman, Zygmunt (2004) *Wasted Lives: Modernity and its Outcasts*, Cambridge: Polity.

Byrd, Johnny 'ByrdDog' (1995) "The Last Mile", *Journal of Prisoners on Prisons*, 6(1): 70-74.

Chevigny, Bell (ed.) (1999) *Doing Time: 25 Years of Prison Writing - A PEN American Center Prize Anthology*, New York: Arcade Publishing, Inc.

Gaucher, Bob (2008) "Carceral Universals", *Journal of Prisoners on Prisons*, 16(2): 1-7.

Gaucher, Bob (ed.) (2002) *Writing As Resistance: The Journal of Prisoners on Prisons Anthology (1988-2002)*, Toronto: Canadian Scholars Press Inc.

Giroux, Henry A. (2009) *Youth in a Suspect Society: Democracy or Disposability?*, New York: Palgrave Macmillan.

Jackson, Michael and Graham Stewart (2009) A Flawed Compass: A Human Rights Analysis of the Roadmap to Strengthening Public Safety, http://www.justicebehindthewalls.net/resources/news/flawed_Compass.pdf.

Mauer, Marc (1999) *Race to Incarcerate*, New York: The New Press.

Mauer, Marc and Meda Chesney-Lind (eds.) (2002) Invisible Punishment: The Collateral Consequences of Mass Imprisonment, New York: The New Press.

EDITOR'S INTRODUCTION

PEN Prison Writing:
Punishment and Creative Resistance
Bell Gale Chevigny

Education in prison reduces recidivism more effectively than any other program; the higher the level of education, the more dramatically recidivism rates drop. Less noted is the salutary effect of arts programs in creative writing, painting, and theater. This issue features work by non-fiction writers who have won prizes in the PEN (Poets, Playwrights, Essayists, Editors, and Novelists) American Center's Prison Writing Program's (PWP) annual literary contest. This nationwide program for writers in prison is the longest-lived and most eminent of its kind.

Since 1960, PEN's Freedom to Write committee has advocated for writers abroad who are persecuted for their writing.[1] But support for saints of free expression abroad does not usually translate into concern for ordinary domestic sinners. Yet in the early 1970s a few members investigated conditions for people writing in U.S. prisons. Learning that federal prisoners were often denied writing materials or free access to mail, they worked to correct those practices. The Attica rebellion and its barbarous repression in 1971 made them want to know more about life behind the walls. And former prisoners "coming out" and speaking eloquently made them wonder about the strengths of others hidden away.[2]

One founder of the PWP, Kathrin Perutz wrote: "To be able to say what you mean, to put in words what you perceive as truth, to impose form on the formless – this is a way to reconstruct a life, to restore a sense of meaning, of responsibility to oneself and to others. But the others – at least, some others – must be listening". To create those listeners, PEN launched the first literary competition for writers in prison in 1973. Men and women incarcerated across the nation submitted entries, some of them emboldened to write for the first time.

The seventies created a "prison renaissance", one man wrote. The Attica rebellion had brought reforms in its wake, and rehabilitation was still a respected goal. Many rich programs were brought to prisons, including college education, arts and writing classes, some funded by the National Endowment for the Arts. Several little magazines emerged, dedicated to publishing work by prisoners.

In the 1980s, support for prison writing plummeted. Ronald Reagan's administration cut financial aid to fledgling magazines, and state funds for programs behind bars evaporated. In 1981, Norman Mailer fought passionately for the release of Jack Abbott, author of the best-selling *In the Belly of the Beast.* Within a month of his release, Abbott killed a man. The romance between convicts and writers had run its course, and interest in prisoners diminished while the victims' rights movement flourished.

PEN's Prison Writing Program almost died in the late eighties. Reader/jurors, always volunteers, fell away, and PEN executives took little interest. Those who valiantly rescued the program, including the late and beloved Fielding Dawson, held the torch in those dark times. We have always had strong supporters, and in this past decade our prestige has grown. To my knowledge no other center of International PEN does anything like this program.

The PWP receives about a thousand manuscripts yearly – in poetry, drama, fiction, essay and memoir – which are read by about twenty of us volunteers working in generic subcommittees.[3] Winners receive modest money awards and our mentor program, initiated by Jackson Taylor, the program's director, offers winners and promising runners-up the opportunity to work with a seasoned writer through correspondence. In these times, prisoners with access to a writing workshop are rare. Incarcerated writers express overwhelming gratitude for the attention the contest represents, and many assert that it has changed their lives.

For PWP members, reading this remarkable work has been at once a privilege and, because of our inability to share it with a larger audience, a burden. Through the years, we have offered public readings of winners' work to enthusiastic, and often astonished, audiences. Writers and actors have done their best to make the winners present, reading in auditoriums, on radio (WBAI and WNYC), and on TV. The video, "Words from the Tiers", produced by Deedee Halleck of Deep Dish TV (www.deepdishtv.org) is often shown on the Free Speech channel. We have also participated in PEN American Center's international literary festivals, World Voices.

In recent years, however, issues like mass incarceration in the U.S., the trend toward imprisoning the mentally ill, the increasingly geriatric prison population, torture by solitary confinement, and capital punishment have made more urgent our desire for a wider audience to experience more directly what only those inside can tell.

With the support of a Soros Senior Justice Fellowship in 1998, I compiled and edited an anthology designed to give ears to the hard of hearing as well as voice to the voiceless; not only, that is, to encourage these isolated writers but also to reveal their humanity, their gifts, and their plight to readers shamefully unaware of them. *Doing Time: 25 Years of Prison Writing,* was published by Arcade in 1999 (paperback in 2000) and is still in print. Instructors in several fields have assigned the book to their students, and it supports the argument for treating works by U.S. prisoners (now a population of 2.3 million), as an important branch of our national literature.[4]

Correspondence and friendships with PEN contest winners continue to educate me and compel me to act on, or share, what I learn. The ways they came to put words to paper in prison and how the writing experience has affected them are for me endlessly moving and illuminating questions.[5] The best prison writing, I have concluded, continues to testify to hidden experience, to critique and resist institutionalization, and it helps writers to find themselves, make themselves whole, forge significant connections with others, make reparations, and meaningfully confront death.[6]

These relationships have drawn me into struggles against the death penalty, for clemency and parole, against cruel and unjust treatment within the walls, for educational help inside and out. The PWP has established an advocacy committee to further these efforts; this committee also helps writers find outlets for their work, through publication and public reading.

The Journal of Prisoners on Prisons (JPP) has published articles by many PEN PWP contest winners – among them Eugene Dey, Charles Huckelbury, and Jon Marc Taylor, and the dedicated and multi-talented late Victor Hassine. The authors in this issue are new to the *JPP*. As the nonfiction pieces sent to us often bear unique witness to outrageous practices, we are glad for the chance to make this work more widely known. This issue is a partial sequel to *Doing Time*.

Justin Piché suggested that, since Canadian penal practices are shifting to the right, partly in imitation of the U.S., this issue might include pieces that reflect some of the more egregious prison conditions in the 'land of the free'. His and Mike Larsen's introduction show how this issue is in part a cautionary one.

Several articles address the punishment that grossly supplements the loss of liberty. Michael Rothwell testifies to suicide in San Quentin. With absurdist humor, Gary T. Carrillo meditates on California's infamous Three

Strikes Law and on suicide among the mentally ill at Vacaville.[7] Christopher Best gives an eyewitness account of Texas' death row at Huntsville. From Vandalia, Missouri, Patricia Prewitt recounts the ironies of contraband rules. A long-termer in Florida's prisons, Charles Norman relates the comic-tragic effects of AIDS behind the walls. William Steed Kelley narrates an example of violence in Texas prisons. These six articles are themselves acts of creative resistance, of course. The next five pieces describe creative resistance directly.

Jorge Renaud's prize-winning essay proposes that outsiders initiate workshops that would help prisoners to think through their lives and learn to give back to their communities. The remaining articles were commissioned for this issue. PEN prize-winning poet Marilyn Buck wrote from federal prison in Dublin, California about the politics of her experience teaching English as a Second Language there. From Bedford Hills Correctional Facility, Judy Clark details the positive rehabilitative effects of the community model of prison that prevailed at the institution for twenty years before the conventional punitive model was restored. Buzz Alexander, the founding genius of the Prison Creative Arts Program (PCAP) in Michigan, wrote the piece about the program to accompany the account of Kinnari Jivani, one of the hundreds of beneficiaries of the initiative, now at Huron Valley State.

This issue also breaks new ground for the *JPP* by presenting the triple testimony of three filmmakers who give voice (and image) through documentry film. Susanne Mason, Katy Chevigny, and Edgar Barens – all engaged in criminal justice issues – recall the ticklish task of gaining access to their subjects. The problem of gaining access to the carceral was a central theme discussed in *JPP* volumes 17(1) and 18 (1&2).

The first three pieces of the Prisoners' Struggles section were ones I commissioned, because I admire the authors and hope their leadership in reform efforts will inspire emulation. Experiences inside of two former prisoners, Anthony Papa and Bruce Reilly, kindled their fire to lead battles for legislative reform – against the Rockefeller Drug Laws and Rhode Island's felon disenfranchisement, respectively. Tamar Kraft-Stolar has no less zeal in leading her Coalition for Women Prisoners in multiple ongoing struggles to important victories for women and their families.

The *JPP*, which shares the mission of the PEN Prison Writing Program to introduce the voices and experiences of prisoners into the conversation, has been very hospitable in dedicating this issue to writers in the PWP. The writers and the committee members are grateful for this opportunity to gain an international audience. We hope that these pieces will stimulate an exchange with people elsewhere who participate in a similar program or are interested in developing one.

ENDNOTES

*   Thanks to my colleagues at PEN, anonymous, hard-working readers of the contest submissions, and to Blue Mountain Center for the Arts for mounting a two and a half-week special issue retreat in May 2009 for artists who are prison activists. This group stimulated ideas for this issue. Old friends – Buzz Alexander, Susanne Mason, Edgar Barens, and Bruce Reilly – gamely supplied essays for it. Jorge Renaud offered editorial assistance.

1   The Writers in Prison program in other countries do the same work.

2   In talk-backs after electrifying productions (in 1967) of "Fortune and Men's Eyes", a play by John Herbert about brutality in a Canadian boy's reformatory, ex-convicts came out of the closet to testify to its veracity. Seeing the need for a forum that would give formerly incarcerated people a voice and provide them with the tools they needed to help rebuild their lives. David Rothenberg, the play's director founded the Fortune Society (see www.fortunesociety.org).

3   See www.pen.org for contest guidelines and for the *Manual for Writers in Prison.* Winning works are also posted on the PEN website.

4   In my view, prisoners' writing is not a genre, but rather the variegated voice of a neglected but significant minority.

5   In *Doing Time,* the biographical sketches of the fifty writers include remarks on these questions.

6   See my essay "'All I Have, A Lament and a Boast': Why Prisoners Write", in *Prose and Cons: Essays on Prison Literature in the United States,* in D. Quentin Miller (2005), Jefferson (NC): McFarland & Company.

7   Mental health treatment can help some prisoners recover from their illness, prevent deterioration, and protect them from suicide. It can encourage the development of more effective internal controls. By helping individual prisoners regain health and improve coping skills, mental health treatment promotes safety and order within the prison environment and enhances community safety when prisoners are ultimately released. Unfortunately, prisons are ill-equipped to respond appropriately to the needs of prisoners with mental illness. Prison mental health services are all too frequently crippled by under-staffing, insufficient facilities, and limited programs. Many seriously ill prisoners receive little or no meaningful treatment. See *Human Rights Watch Statement for the Record to the Senate Judiciary Committee Subcommittee on Human Rights and the Law*, September 22, 2009.

ABOUT THE SPECIAL ISSUE EDITOR

Professor Emerita of Literature at SUNY, Purchase College, *Bell Gale Chevigny* has been a member of the PEN Prison Writing Committee since 1993 (Chair from 2002-2005). She also serves on the board of Prison Legal News as well as the Advisory Boards of PEN, Prison Creative Arts Project, and Resist. With Open Society Institute support, she edited *Doing Time: 25 Years of Prison Writing,* A PEN American Center Prize Anthology (Arcade, 1999). She initiated the PWP's Advocacy Committee. Chevigny has taught writing workshops in prisons and among ex-prisoners. She has lectured widely and written frequently about writers in prison. Fifteen writers in *Doing Time* have joined her for shared readings all over the United States. Among her publications are three other books, some short fiction, and many articles on social issues and artists.

Check Out Day
Michael Rothwell

There's always a way out of prison, any prison, and it can be done right now, today. The authorities can't stop you. Well, they can slow you down if you're careless, but they really can't stop you if you're determined enough.

It's called "checking out", or "taking it to the vent", or even "moving on to the next phase". Sometimes I think about the guys that were with me when I first came into prison who are no longer here. And I'm not talking about paroling. Some are gone from disease – a few to cancers and a couple more to heart attacks – but the vast majority were done in by their own hand.

I think the all time winner for originality would have to be Ben. He was a neighbor of mine in Folsom that lived a few doors down, and I spoke to him a few days before he left. We were talking law, and he was trying to explain the "doctrine of laches" to me. It has to do with time constraints in getting your criminal case back to court. It was all but gibberish to me, so I pressed Ben, who was a well regarded jailhouse lawyer, to help me deal with this issue of "laches".

I'll never forget the faraway look in his eyes as he told me he had something coming up that would prevent him from aiding me with my legal work. My initial reaction was that I thought he was having trouble with someone, and fixing to get in some sort of wreck which would likely result with him ending up in the hole – a common enough occurrence in these places.

I told him that whatever the problem was, I'd take care of it one way or another. I really needed to get over this legal hurdle to having my appeal heard, and I needed someone who, unlike myself, knew what they were doing. Again, I got that thousand yard stare, and he said, "No, it's not that. It's just a personal thing I have to deal with". Right there, that should have been my first clue. But my attitude was, whatever, if he wasn't going to help me, then I could accept no, and I immediately began focusing on other avenues to get my legal work done.

I didn't give another thought about what Ben had said until a couple of days later when I was at work in the Watch Office and a call came in that there had been a suicide in my cellblock. The office I worked in was between the cellblock and the Infirmary where they would take any dead body, so I knew I'd get a good look at whoever it was as they wheeled the corpse on by. It was Ben. His last words to me now made perfect sense. He definitely had something else on his mind, all right.

As a clerk, I would type and process all the reports involving any "incident", such as a suicide, in the facility. What Ben did was take an ordinary electrical extension cord and cut it in two with toenail clippers. Still using the clippers, he stripped the insulation back a few inches on both ends where the wire had been cut. On the half that didn't plug into the wall, he took most of the rest of the insulation off, and wrapped it around himself. He put a wet washcloth in his mouth – I always wondered if that made any difference – and slugged the other half into the wall socket, but without touching the now live end to the one he was wrapped up in so it didn't complete the circuit.

After that, he lay down on his bunk with both exposed ends of the wire in hand and then held them together. I found out later from one of the guys that worked in the library that Ben had been studying all the books dealing with electricity he could find. He had rather ingeniously figured out how to wrap himself up in a way that didn't trip the circuit breaker as he was gradually cooked.

I thought about how many times I've been shocked, for just a second or two, by an electrical outlet. Maybe a dozen times, give or take, when carelessly changing a light bulb without unplugging it first or what have you. It's not a pleasant feeling, but it's sure not going to kill you right away either. Ben had to actually hold those wires together as he was slow-roasted by the 120 volts. That's determination.

By the time they got his remains to the Infirmary, which was several minutes after they found him, his core body temperature was still well over 120 degrees, at least that was as high as their thermometer went. Flesh literally flayed off his bones like the meat off a rack of well done spare ribs. Later, a bad joke on the yard was that you could stick a fork in him – he was done.

Another guy I knew, Dusty, got the job done without as much finesse, but still got to where he wanted to go. I had known Dusty for some time and watched him parole out of prison twice. The final time he came in was with a multiple Three Strike sentence, I think it was 75 years to life, and I reckon Dusty had had enough. He never hurt anyone that I knew of. He was pretty much your run-of-the-mill drug addict who stole money to feed his disease.

He lay down on his bunk when his cellie was gone and positioned himself sideways with his legs up on the wall and his head hanging over the side to insure the blood would rush towards his brain. He cut his jugular vein with a razor blade, and bled out quickly. He left behind quite a mess, but at that point I don't guess he cared much.

They usually transfer us around to different prisons every few years or so, and during my tenure with the Department of Corrections so far I've seen too many check outs to recount here. Suffice to say that most guys who choose to go out that way simply "hang it up". Braided strips of torn sheets work just fine. A lot of guys don't even bother to braid them. There's always a vent handy or in the old prisons, like San Quentin, bars on the front of the cells that will do nicely. And it was there in San Quentin, that I witnessed my most memorable suicide.

It was Christmastime, but the season of joy for much of the world often turned into deep depression for some of the denizens of that gothic "Bastille by the Bay", especially in the hole, where I was serving a "SHU" (Security Housing Unit) term for being caught in possession of a weapon. Other than a few hours a week on a tiny yard you were locked in your four by nine foot cell virtually all the time. Whenever you came out of your cell you were cuffed up and under police escort. It was in the SHU that I began to fully appreciate what the term "stir crazy" meant. I certainly noticed it in the people around me.

Folsom prison, of Johnny Cash fame, is nicknamed "Dracula's Castle" by the convicts in California. I always thought San Quentin should be dubbed "Frankenstein's Laboratory". Built primarily in the 19th century, everything there is old and colored in cheerless shades of grey. It looked, and living there felt, like something out of a bygone era.

At the time, Donner Section in South Block was pretty much the end of the line for the guys who had gotten in trouble for one thing or another throughout California's other state prisons, and it also served to house the overflow for the condemned from Death Row. Donner Section filled only a quarter of South Block, but it was still enormous. Five tiers high and 50 cells across it were built in the fashion of traditional prison architecture from a century or so ago. San Quentin and Folsom were California's original prisons, with each of their main cellblocks designed as "a building inside a building". The inner building was constructed in the form of a large block honeycombed with a lattice of cells and infrastructure. Another building, which is basically a shell enclosing the block of cells, was supposed to serve as a barrier against the elements, but usually the temperature inside was the same as the outside. On the inside of this outer shell, at heights equal to the cellblock's 3rd and 5th tier, were catwalks for a guard who always carried a rifle, and who had a fairly panoramic view of several cells and tiers at any given point. That outer shell kept most of the rain out, but for those of us destined to spend our days bound in prison culture, it's the inner cellblock where our lives' dramas play out.

There was reading, "fishing" (passing items via handmade lines from cell to cell), and exercise (lots of pushups) to spend one's time; but you had to be on guard, for Death stalked those ancient tiers. Clinical depression was what could give the Reaper the key to your cell. Don't say it couldn't happen to you. Better not to tempt fate. You had to always be on guard against succumbing to conditions that can spawn a state of mind so foul it can cause a young man in the prime of life to want to leave this realm. No matter how upbeat you may feel, there's always a part of you that's miserable. If not, then there's something really wrong with you.

Make no mistake about it, prison is punishment. People suffer. People die. Months and years in that kind of environment can twist anyone's mind to some degree. I don't think it's a matter of just staying strong; I think it's more a matter of never letting your guard down. Don't let it get to you. You have to be vigilant to keep that inner demon at arm's length. It's always going to be there, so you better learn to keep it at bay. One way is to keep doing those pushups. They help.

The cops are supposed to patrol the tiers a little more often during the Yultide season because people do get more down than usual. But if someone's determined to check out, then there's not much they can do about it. And that's exactly what happened one dreary December night.

I noticed some activity by the three block cops up on the 3rd tier evidenced by the jingling of keys and reflection of their shadows moving on the outer wall. The gunner on one of the catwalks had spotted something that caused him to raise the alarm. A Sergeant and Lieutenant strolled in a few minutes later and trudged up the stairs towards the 3rd tier. Everyone knew something had happened when the brass actually walked the tier. The Sergeant and Lieutenant left after a minute or two, and then a couple of the cops walked slowly back down the stairs towards the fiberglass Stokes stretcher located on the 1st tier that hung on the outer wall in plain view of the cells. Their younger counterpart remained on the 3rd tier by the cell in question. The two cops getting the bright orange stretcher were taking their sweet time, obviously trying to eat up the rest of their watch. At that point, I still wasn't sure if there had been an actual death in the block, but I knew something was up. Be it a sprained ankle, stroke or suicide, I figured the speed of their response would be about the same.

There's an old saying I heard long before I ever got there that goes, "If you want to see the scum of the earth, just go to San Quentin . . . " and, after a pause, "at shift change". This is an old saw familiar in virtually all penal institutions out West, and these two cops fit the description of a couple of grizzled old bulls. They looked like they'd been there for decades, and their demeanor suggested that they had seen it all. The removal of a carcass, whether dead or alive, was just one less body they had to deal with that shift. In other words, business as usual.

Hushed talk snaked its' way down through the block. There was indeed a suicide on the 3rd tier. I lived just a couple of cells down from the entrance on the 1st tier, and like with Ben, it was the perfect place for viewing the body, as they had to go right past me to exit the cellblock.

But unlike the fictitious laboratory where unholy life was created in the Frankenstein story, on this very real dark and stormy night San Quentin claimed another victim. The prison itself, or more precisely the conditions there, killed another human being just as sure as if, under its own volition, it had dropped one of its medieval bricks off a wall onto somebody's head. Except the "Q" was much more subtle about it than that.

The whispers started as they always do whenever there's a suicide. "What a weak punk", and variations thereof, were voiced by a few. It happens every time, without fail. It's like the guys who say it are trying to convince themselves it could never happen to them. As if they're better than that. But you can always hear the fear in their voices, no matter how hard they try to cover it up. Every time. As if bad mouthing the dead would prevent anyone, who's in that dark frame of mind, from "doing" themselves.

I think there is a much better way, however, to break just about anyone from ever contemplating taking the "easy" way out. Because, from the suicides I've seen, there isn't anything easy about it, and this was perhaps the ultimate case in point.

A few minutes later the old screws sauntered down the tier with their gruesome cargo, carrying the stretcher head first on either side with the younger cop helping balance the rear of it. It was like they were taking a leisurely walk in the park. No hurry getting this dead body out of there at all and I wondered if they did this on purpose. Maybe they wanted us to get a good look at him, because he was completely uncovered, naked except for the skivvies he had on, along with the homemade "scarf" he still had wrapped around his neck. Or maybe that old saying about the cops there was true. I don't know. But I do know that the cat I saw on the stretcher looked like he was about 19 years old and a young 19 at that. He would have looked more in place at a high school dance that night rather than being carried out of the hole dead in San Quentin prison.

For the first time in my life I fully understood the term "death mask". The handmade noose around his neck consisted of sloppily braided strips of sheet, and his head was bent at an impossible angle in relation to his shoulders.

Evidently, he had been hanging for a while because rigor mortis had set in. He must have changed his mind about his final life decision that night because both hands were at his neck, as though he tried to undo the fix he found himself in while the last vestige of his consciousness ebbed into eternity. His attempts to ease what must have been the ever tightening grip on his throat had obviously failed, but had caused his fingers to get trapped between the makeshift rope and his neck. Both elbows stuck out rigidly locked in place and told the story of the losing battle that played out during the last moments of his life. His eyes were half open, and mouth curled back in a horrible grimace . . . the "death mask".

At that moment my mind flashed back to an image of a couple of stillborn puppies out of our dog's litter when I was 4 or 5 years old. It was the first time I had seen death in a mammal. The stillness emanating from those semi-closed puppy eyes looked almost exactly the same as what I saw coming from the dead guy's eyes in front of me. The total and absolute stillness of the eyes. You would think common decency would dictate any first responder to at least shut the eyes of a dead man, but not so there. Witnessing this was perhaps the best possible cure for anyone in a depressing situation that might entertain the thought of suicide. I don't care how bad I feel, or how hopeless the situation might seem – I don't ever want to look like that.

Homeboy made a bad choice that night. He tried to reverse the decision he made, but unlike a lot of us who, at one time or another in our lives screw up royally, and deservedly or not, get another chance – he didn't. He tempted fate, but fate was in no mood to be fooled with that night. The cops went out and slammed the steel door shut behind them as they made their way to the prison morgue.

Not ten minutes later they were back. It was as quiet in that huge cellblock as it ever was. You could almost hear the mice scampering across the cold concrete floors. Usually there were various types of yelling at all hours around the clock; conversations between cells on different tiers, chess games hollered back and forth between cells with moves called out on numbered squares, and guys casting their fishlines out over the tier and shouting to their intended recipients "Can you see my line yet?" Or just the senseless babble the nuts spew out in order to validate their existence. Bedlam was a good name for it on a normal day. But not right then. There was only solemn silence. Even the crazy guys had shut up.

For the first time since I was there, I could actually hear the footsteps of the two old cops echoing through the cavernous cellblock as one of them, carrying the now light Stokes stretcher, hung it back up on the wall. With a bit of a dramatic flair, he turned towards the convicts in their cells. It was as though he was on stage facing a giant vertical amphitheater – San Quentin's version of the Hollywood Bowl. He had everyone's complete attention. It was so still, the proverbial dropped pin would have sounded like a gunshot going off. Was he going to say a few kind words about the recently deceased? Maybe warn us about the dangers of unchecked depression? A short lecture, perhaps, to be careful lest one of us ever lands the lead role in this tragedy?

The old bull, who obviously relished his time in the spotlight and milked the silence as well as any Tony Award winning Broadway actor, stood there for several seconds slowly scanning the tiers that held his rapt audience. Then, before he walked away laughing with his buddy, just one word bellowed out of his mouth loud enough for the inhabitants of all 250 cells to hear, "Next!".

ABOUT THE AUTHOR

Michael Rothwell was born and raised in Los Angeles County. In 1981, he was convicted of second degree murder for shooting one of two men that broke into his home, and was sentenced to 22 years to life. Winning

First Place in the PEN American Center's nonfiction category in 2008 for "Check Out Day", changed his life, he says. He had always been told that he has a knack for writing, but never took it seriously; now he is writing constantly. He has recently completed his first novel, *After the Fall*, "a post-apocalyptical thrill ride through what was once the United States"; he is actively seeking a publisher. He has been the ping-pong champion at Folsom, San Quentin, and Soledad Prisons, and he recently had a six-year winning streak pitching for the Creekside Dodgers. He will be happy to answer all mail from anyone who found *Check Out Day* interesting.

Michael Rothwell #C-10513, B-9-213U
MCSP
P.O. Box 409040
Ione, CA 95640

In Good Company
Gary T. Carrillo

Homelessness is an insane situation which many people try to escape through drinking and drugs. Once the feeling of hopelessness sets in, it's only a matter of time before a person seeks food or shelter on his own terms. This is why, for one reason or another, many homeless people end up in jail or prison.

The following stories deal with homeless people after they are taken off the street – after you can't see them anymore. I have told them with humor because I believe that laughter can heal many wounds. One wound I'd like to see healed is the disposal of promising lives, thrown away through laws such as Three Strikes.

* * *

GOMER

When I first arrived on the psych unit of the San Diego County Jail, I noticed that the atmosphere was much quieter than in the mainline. . .

I remember one of my first breakfasts on the psych unit. A big, goofy looking dude, asked, "Hey, anybody want these eggs?"

"No", I said.

"Hey Gomer, want these eggs?" He was talking to a guy who looked a lot like Gargamel from the Smurfs.

"What it mean, dis 'Gomer?'", asked Gargamel.

"Well, it's a figure of speech", dude said in full Southern drawl. "It means pencil neck geek".

The whole table erupted in laughter. I guess it seemed funny because it was so unexpected.

That was the beginning of my journey through absurdity, tomfoolery, grab-ass shenanigans. I needed the comic relief because all I could think about was killing myself.

* * *

BREAKFAST WITH A TWIST

Part of the thrill of suicide is brandishing it in other people's faces. The audience: yes, what every great drama needs. And it's a rush to perform.

Perhaps that's why a young man was now hanging by his neck from the second tier. Damn! He even had a plastic bag over his head just to be sure! The only problem was that the sheriff deputies were now cutting him down and roughing him up at the same time!

He looked like an astronaut from some other planet with his bubble-like breathing apparatus and the white cord connecting him to the mother ship. Who were these alienesque hostiles, trying to waylay this cuckoo cosmonaut?

For several days he had been walking around with a slipknot around his neck like a tie. And just last week we were lining up for breakfast and here comes cuckoo cosmonaut. He pauses at the top of the stairs, then without warning does a nose-dive – BAM BAM BANG! – down the entire flight. Then he stands up like nothing happened. "I'm OK", he says, and proceeds to eat his breakfast.

All he got was a black eye!

* * *

MAKING THE CUT

I've made the cut. I am in the psych tank shower at the brand new Central Jail. I hope I've found a vein large enough to keep bleeding as long as I run hot water over the wound.

I am standing in that shower for half an hour. Damn! It isn't working. People in the day room are getting suspicious. I wrap the cut in toilet paper, and run the water for a few more minutes to wash the blood down the drain. Hell! I'll try again later. I am relieved that I am still alive, yet frustrated that my feeble attempt didn't work.

Light-headed, I make it down the stairs and across the dayroom to my cell. Feeling suspicious. Very suspicious. I'm thinking that everyone knows what I did, even the guard in the control tower.

I am feeling very ugly inside. And I am feeling relief that I took action. I know that I will do it again. I thought God wasn't supposed to give me more than I can handle. This is too much, way too much for me to handle. Now I know I have to die, and it will be good. Screw them. I am not going to serve their sentence. I did not do anything to deserve 39 to life. I would rather die than serve a life sentence I don't deserve.

* * *

DISORDER IN THE COURT

I can't believe the probation officer just knocked over the water jug from the D.A.'s desk onto the floor! I'm not laughing, though. This is way too serious.

It's understandable that the probation officer should be flustered, after delivering that bipolar pre-sentence report. I'm looking at it now...Hmmm... "Mr. Carrillo claims to have been taken from his mother at an early age (8 or 9), and then moved around between 20 or 30 foster placements... drug and alcohol problems... none of this has been corroborated... Anyway, these mitigating circumstances will not be considered, as this is a three strikes case ... blah... blah... blah".

Then the little chipmunk D.A. chirps up, "Do the crime, do the time", in her best Mary Poppins meets Cathy Bates voice.

No wonder I'm going crazy.

The P.O. had the nerve to tell me that she sympathized with the nature of my upbringing, as she used to be a child social worker. But, it's now "her job" to sentence me to the maximum: 39 to life. Gee, thanks for your sympathy.

My third strike: assault with a deadly weapon. I cut a guy's hand in a fight at the homeless shelter. Yeah, the wound required stitches. He had threatened to kick my ass and have me shot. My right hand was broken and in a cast at the time. I guess that brought out the bravado in him.

Now the D.A. has her PowerPoint projector setup. Never at a loss for words, she says to the jury, "I have to admit this is probably my third time using PowerPoint... if the projector blows up, I'll try to aim it at the Public Defender!" She is gonna catch hell at the next D.A. / Parole Department. / Judge barbecue.

* * *

SLASH

Instead of going to court, I decided to slash my wrist. My cellie threw up. Then he called for the sheriff's deputies over the intercom.

I received stitches along with a brace – which they then took from me – to keep the damaged tendons from snapping. I spent the night in a padded safety cell with a grate in the floor for a bathroom. 1 was wearing a thick Fred Flintstone get-up.

The doctor came to talk to me in the morning, then released me to the acute care unit. There I met some interesting characters. "Cut Throat" had earned his name by cutting his throat from ear to ear with a razor blade. "Mogley" was a dead ringer for the jungle boy. "Spider Man" had slashed both arteries in his wrists and sprayed blood just like the super hero sprays webs.

Cuckoo Cosmonaut was also in the acute unit. This time he was wearing a massive cast which extended from his shoulder to his hand. He had jumped off the tier head first. Earlier that week someone else had died performing the same maneuver.

I asked Cuckoo Cosmonaut why he wanted to kill himself.

"Well, I don't anymore, now that I see you and other people here looking at life sentences".

"What are you facing?", I asked him.

"Six months".

"How else have you tried to kill yourself?"

"I tried to drown myself in the toilet – I thought the urine would kill me".

ABOUT THE AUTHOR

Gary T. Carrillo, born in Escondido, is serving a 39-to-life under California's Three Strikes and You're Out law. He did not kill anyone. He asserts he cut someone on the hand. This is only his second time in prison. He won second prize in the PEN American Center's memoir in 2004. "In Good Company" drew on his experiences in the Department of Mental Health in Vacaville State Prison in California. "I am doing better than I ever have while serving this sentence – still laughing at the absurdities of human nature," he writes, "my own included". A lifer now at New Folsom (California State Prison in Sacramento), he reports that these psych programs basically saved his life: "What matters is what's in your heart. And if you can look into your heart and find something good, if you can find love—for life and all its creatures—then you can call that God. And you'll be alright regardless of what hell you find yourself in".

LIVE! From Texas Death Row
Christopher J. Best

I just got off work. I hate my job. I never want to go back, but it's not an option. I can't quit and I can't get fired. I'm a Texas prisoner and I work on death row.

I'm what Texas calls a Support Service Inmate (SSI). In plain talk, I'm a state-approved janitor. The guys on death row used to clean up their own place, but after an escape and a hostage-taking incident the condemned stay locked down. They bring in a few of us short-timers from GP, general population. I'm not proud to say I'm doing a few years for beating up my ex for cheating.

My first day on my death row job was hell, just like each day since. New canvas shoes, called "state shoes", had just come in to unit supply and my work partners and I passed them out. The three of us – me, Hallman and an older gay dude they call Cherry-Pop – each took a tier, going cell to cell with the shoes. Every last sensory-deprived inmate had something to say from inside his matchbox.

"Hey! White boy! Can a nigga get some shoes?!"

"Yo! What's for last chow?!"

"Look out, SSI! Tell that law they didn't gimme no shower yet!"

Cherry-Pop is especially popular. In prison lingo, "she" is a long-time "punk", as they call 'em. They used to call her Cherry, but then her teeth started falling out, which suits some of her death-row clients just fine. "Tell Cherry-Pop dat C-love wanna holla at her", insisted one. When a punk is the object of attention it's not something you'd want to pass your eyelids.

As we worked, I felt obligated to respond to everyone. For these guys, it seems every request is like their last. I quickly fell behind my co-workers on the rows above and below me. Each run is segmented by doors on hinges, which serve as traffic barriers in case some dude is "accidentally" let out of his cell or somehow pops his own cell door. All the cell doors on death row and in GP are on rails, and I wasn't used to dealing with a door on hinges. It's funny what we take for granted, things like forks, ballpoint pens that work, fresh fruit – all such things we do without in here – and doors on hinges.

As I was hurrying to catch up I put a little too much elbow into one of those doors. It flew closed, like a sideways guillotine. BAM! All the chatter instantly stopped. Silence. A fraction of a second later a voice bellowed out, "You motherfuckin' ho! Come slam that door again, you unstan' me?!"

I had just violated death row sanctity, peace and privacy – what little there is of it. Death row has its many rules, and making noise louder than them is a violation of one of them. My face burned with the realization, but only for a moment. It then occurred to me that every death row prisoner on C-Pod had just heard me get talked to like a little bitch. A different kind of burn came over me. I passed out a couple of more pairs of state shoes, until I came to the next door. Being the mature dude I am, I slammed it as hard as I could. *BAAMMM!!* C-Pod reverberated with my rage. Echoes descended into a second or two of utter silence.

The place exploded. Screaming. Banging. Whistling. Threats. My Momma was fondly remembered. There was end-of-the-world metal-on-metal grating and clanging, like an earthquake. The surge of instant unity and noise brought in a rush of guards. We dropped the boxes of state shoes and were escorted off C-Pod. It all happened so fast that the internees had no time to prepare their usual punishment: piss and shit bombs.

Word travels fast, even out of what is supposed to be one of the worlds most secure institutions. When I left the job and got back to my minimum-security cell on the other side of the prison, three known gang members approached me. Their spokesman didn't waste words. "What's your fuckin' problem, *guero*? You wanna die?"

"What are you talking about?"

"Oh, now you wanna play games? You slammin' doors on death row!"

Shit. This is fucked up, I thought. There was only one way to resolve this confrontation like a man. "I don't know what you're talking about". The look in his eyes, and undoubtedly the look in mine, said different.

"He got the message", maestro told his henchmen, his gaze still locked on me. It took three days for the ruckus to simmer down, both on death row and in GP. Not bad for my first day at work, huh? Only a handful of death threats. I stayed off C-Pod as much as possible from then on.

From my view in here, death out there now looks relatively easy. For freeworld folks, death is merely a passage, or a rite, or a transient thing among all the life-stuff. Most people have the freedom to push life's most sensitive and controversial issue out of their minds, or at least deal with it conventionally and on their own terms: family tradition, discussions, plans, a last will and testament, maybe an estate, or to hell with it all and let's watch the next game on TV.

In the penitentiary, especially on death row, Moloch calls all the shots. Looking at it every day, living with it every day, is a perpetual, real-life nightmare – the kind only men at their worst can foist on one another, call it Andersonville, the Hanoi Hilton, Abu Ghraib or the Texas pen.

You may know that, as governor, President Bush signed 147 death warrants, more than any American since the death penalty was reinstated by the Supreme Court in 1976. No one need wonder where the culture of depravity and love of death surrounding Abu Ghraib comes from. It was born in Texas, where O. Lane McCotter was once the state prison director.[1]

Institutionalists argue which came first, the bad prisoner "eggs" or the bad guard "chickens". It took both. No man goes to prison in Texas for singing too loud in church, at least not until the next round of expansion, which implies that good prisoners are made, not born. Bad guards don't give men a chance to adjust to incarcerated life, which is critically important for the young demographic classified to Terrell. When the rule of law is meaningless to overseers, prisoners begin to think the system is unjust, including the Constitution. They turn to "family".

The computer tracks every convict by code. When an prisoner dies in custody, by legal or illegal execution or by natural causes, his status is recorded as "DX". He's Dead, X-ed out, like flattened cartoon characters with Xs on their eyes. It's the supreme "cross-out", to use the convict term for elimination. X-it, stage left.

Code "DX" allows the prison system to "clear count", conducted every two hours, assuring that all prisoners, dead or alive, are (supposedly) accounted for. The coding is a small cog in the sanitized machinery of death, distancing government employees from blood and its consequences in much the same, impersonal way a criminal shoots his victim and flees the scene. The mess and the tragedy are left for someone else.

This process of death-by-government is also distinctly American. It's an odd mix of bureaucracy and market-based specialization. The system preserves itself by appealing to our baser instincts while employing the latest technology and carefully measured political trends. Thus, the Supreme Court keeps fine-tuning the mechanism of death, as the late justice Harry Blackmum once critiqued. Capitalism is neither moral nor immoral but proceeds according to its practitioners; the immoral version keeps revising the supposedly constitutional basis of the death penalty by extra-constitutional opinion polls, tests borrowed from international law, and so on. It's a fraud, of course, not restricted to the death penalty question.

Every day I confront blood and its consequences. Every day I struggle to keep my own life-force contained and flowing, beating back, cajoling, and deceiving Moloch away from my doorposts. As I tell you about it, the names herein have been changed to protect the living, the dead and to keep my ass from getting shanked. As a worker on death row, I am a member of the death society. Each of us has our own way of dealing with death. Our society is nothing more than the human condition writ large and bold, condensed in time and drama, pressed by unrelenting dark forces, often relieved by the sweetest of human kindness, foibles and even the occasional angel in disguise.

My SSI job evolved from the old building tender job that existed for many years before the *Ruiz v. Estelle* court decrees of a quarter-century ago. BTs carried the big, brass keys, swept and mopped the corridors and dayrooms, and administered justice at the end of a broom or mop handle or with those keys – any which way they could. These days the SSIs are caught between the guard and the convicts but without the brutal leverage of the old BTs. Guards recruit the SSIs as snitches, often by coercion, and prisoners try to take advantage of the SSIs' freedom of movement. Peer pressure and ostracization and threats are common. These problems are magnified on death row.

Each morning when I arrive at work, I hand my ID card to a guard at the building entrance. I swear, lately I have come to smell and taste the death-row building even before I step inside. As I walk in, I *feel* the dread on my flesh, even in me. Next comes the strip search, the ubiquitous humiliation of prison life, also magnified on death row because it's conducted with much more detail. My co-workers and I remove every stitch of clothing. One guard carefully inspects each clothing item, turning socks, boxers, pants, and shirt inside-out, inspecting seams for hidden items, crinkling every square inch of fabric. Our shoes are bent, unlaced, pounded, and tossed, insoles left here and there on the floor.

Next, each of us spreads our legs, opens our butt cheeks, shows the bottoms of our feet, holds up our package of manhood, opens our mouth, and turns all about, arms held high. Next, each of us sits on a metal-detecting chair, which looks at our guts with some sort of high-tech imaging, to make sure we haven't swallowed a weapon or contraband. Finally, we place our faces on a metal-detecting plate on the wall, first one side then the other, as a double-check on the mouth. From this point and all day long, a series of cameras bear down on us in all the hallways, and guards stationed at a series of gates check all movement and action.

My first chore is to pick up five or six buggies of clothes that have been wheeled in from the prison's laundry. I separate it all: boxers, socks, jumpsuits and towels, with sheets and pillowcases every Wednesday. A few years ago TDCJ prided itself on the fact that, for all its other troubles, the men got fresh, clean clothes every day. No more. The system is constantly cutting the budget as Texas goes broke supporting its criminal-justice apparatus. All prisoners receive "clean" clothes every other day – shirt and pants in GP, jumpsuits for death row and administrative prisoners (the bad actors). The clothes and linens are always dingy from infrequent washing, prisoner theft of bleach and soap, and from unsupervised machine operators who cut short washing cycles to get out of work. Staph infection is rampant. Guys who can afford it buy and wash their own socks, boxers, T-shirts and commissary detergent.

All day long we see death-row prisoners being escorted here and there, to medical appointments, or to see lawyers or other visitors. Each escort consists of two guards, and the prisoner is handcuffed behind his back. Each guard carries a baton and at least one of them has pepper gas. Some of the cons on death row hang their heads low when they walk. Their time draws near. Others seem almost chipper. They smile, perhaps on their way to visitation. Some guards respond well to the guys, joking and chatting if it seems appropriate, or quiet and all-business if the dude is sullen or dejected.

Like the head, the feet also tell the story on the row. Prisoners who can't afford the $38 white Converse tennies wear state shoes or slippers. All state gear makes a lot more noise. You can tell the mood of the prisoner by the sound of his shuffle in state shoes or slippers. *Shh-shh-ssst*, goes the dragging feet of a downer. *Clip-clop-clap*, patters the buoyant man's prance in his plastic-shorn, high-steppin' feet. He's "trying to get somewhere", as they say in here, and today it's not the needle.

Our local death society is a building full of folks waiting to move onto the next stage of their lives: death. Methods of coping range from quiet meditation to anti-death penalty activism, from good and bad writ-writing to the other kinds of appeal to Higher Law. There is ministry. There is gang activity. There is every shade of selfish, and generous motivation and act.

Hector, for example, arrived on death row in 1999. The only things in his cell were a mattress and pillow, sheathed in hard, crinkly Texas Department of Criminal Justice mattress factory blue plastic, a couple of stained sheets and an even blacker pillowcase, a small and virtually useless cell towel, a partial roll of toilet paper and a prickly wool blanket. At that time, death row inhabitants worked the jobs. One of them was sweeping the run when he came to Hector's cell. "Whadda they call ya, new-boot?"

Hector told him and the worker stepped back from his cell door so he could be seen from all three tiers. He hollered to everyone, "New man here!" An hour later the worker returned, saying nothing this time but clandestinely sweeping a brown paper bag into Hector's cell. Hector guardedly opened the bag and peered in. He found stamps, envelopes, a notepad, pen, soap, shampoo, toothpaste, a toothbrush, a Dolly Madison pastry, a can of Big Red soda and a pack of Ramen noodles.

"That was the last thing I expected", Hector told me. "They did that for a stranger". He continued, "What did I find in that sack? I found care. I found kindness, love, compassion and humanity". Hector told me this story as he finished adding his small contribution to a new paper bag. He tossed it to the floor, to be swept into the house of the newest member of the death society.

One day an unfamiliar dude beckoned me again and again. I tried to ignore him but he was persistent. As I worked my way closer to his cell, trying to pass myself off as genuinely busy, he began a stammering whisper.

"H—h—hey, man. C—c—come 'ere. I, I g—got ten stamps". Stamps are a universal currency in the pen. He was offering me the standard fee on the row to have something moved. In GP, prisoners move items for little or nothing – maybe fifty cents. The intensive security of death row is a more risky and thus more lucrative market. I peered into his cell window and saw a short, bald guy, perhaps 60, with a round face and chubby, chipmunk cheeks. He put his face right up next to mine.

"H-h—hey. Can -- can you go get *s-s—s* . . . can you go get s—something for me? I got, I got ten stamps". He kept looking behind him, his eyes darting all around his empty cell. I liked this guy already. He was entertainment in a place where little is found.

I went to the cell he told me about. "Psst", out slides a brown sack with so little in it that it looked like trash. Good. Easy to move. I shuttled it under Chipmunk's door.

"You wanna, you wanna d—do s—something else?" More easy stamps. I got to thinking about this little adventure. What was this guy up to? From the other cell another sack shot out – it seemed empty. Curiosity won out. I picked it up and carefully looked inside. It was a little batch of clipped toenails or fingernails! I dropped it in disgust and angrily swept it along and slapshot it into Chipmunk's house.

"You motherfucker!", I charged.

"What the hell you got me into with this sick stuff?"

Chipmunk turns and retrieves three paper bags from under his bunk. He pours them out on his metal cell table. There's a pile of what looks to be two or three pounds of fingernails and toenails. He looks me straight in the eye and smiles pleasantly and says, "S-s-smells like hot dogs".

It turns out old Chipmunk was sending the nails out to his sister, who was packaging and selling them on the Internet as artifacts from mass murderers. The world is full of sickos and they're not all in the penitentiary. I later learned the Texas Legislature was so disturbed over this kind of thing that they passed a new law forbidding death row prisoners from selling body hair, nails, fluids and what-ever else they could peel off themselves. Chipmunk was right about one thing. Those damn nails did smell like hot dogs.

Texas Department of Criminal Justice (TDCJ) guards are reluctant members of the death society. For most of them it's just a job, they tell you. And later, they tell you again. There is a certain camaraderie among prison guards you'd expect, especially on violent farms where there's a siege mentality. On death row that camaraderie is more close-knit, binding employees with support-group activities, on and off the job. They hold potluck lunches and suppers on the row – "spreads", as any penitentiary potluck is called – breaking bread in solidarity. They have their own body language and terminology, mostly affirming, feel-good stuff. It's homemade therapy to get them through "just a job".

Most do a good job. A few do a "nothing" job. Fewer still are rotten to the core: haters. Administrators use them to stir things up and manipulate prison policy. One bum in gray has identified his mark, one of the death row guys with some property. The mulligan is trying to get next to the dude so maybe he will get a cut of the estate after the execution. He treats the rest of us like dirt. Speaking of dirt, most of the haters in gray claim to be law-and-order types, but they're also the ones bringing in most of the contraband and breaking other rules.

Some guards do all they can to humanize death row and beat back death's descent with small favors. Maybe it takes the form of a piece of Texas pecan pie. Cigarettes were outlawed several years ago, but some of the guys who get real close to their dates have a last smoke or two. The best guards avoid the pettiness of the bureaucracy.

Most convicts on death row understand the guards have to make a living. A few men hate everything in gray, almost as a matter of revolutionary principle. It's a sick kind of hate that also extends to society and America as well as all the symbols of the West and freedom. The vast majority of these guys are guilty as sin and the vileness of their crimes continues in a bitterness toward everything human.

Some of the guys appreciate the guards as their only glimpse of free society: What did you watch on TV last night? Did Guns 'n Roses ever release that album? Did your kid pass his math test? What does that new low-carb beer taste like? Every answer or response plied from the keepers is an affirmation of everyone's humanity. It's reciprocal. It's vital.

The more I work here, the more my barriers toward America's forsaken come down. On days when I am the only human a death row prisoner interacts with, it affects me as well as him. He understands that my time with him is short, so he'll often cram as much conversation as possible into mere minutes. It's not that he's in a hurry to die; he's in a hurry to live to the fullest. He won't just tell you his life story, he'll plead it. He desperately seeks some understanding. If I give him that, then the whole world has done the same.

Forty-seven days before his execution date, Reece shares his being. "I've thought many a night about what happens after death", he begins, like many before him. "I can't help but feel there is consciousness after death, but I don't know exactly what's waiting for me. What you don't know can be scary. It's been giving me some wild dreams", I've heard this, too, I was thinking. Then Reece departed from the script. "You know, nothing compares to the fear, and the hurt, when I look in my Daddy's eyes". I look at Reece – something I normally avoid in these sessions. His bottom lip is shivering. His eyes are teary and he turns away from me.

"I got a peace about dying", he says. "I really do". It occurs to me that I am listening to Reece's last meaningful words. He turns to me again, eyes wiped. "My Daddy visits a lot more than he used to. We're close. Tight – is that what they say nowadays?" He laughs faintly. "This is my third date they've set. Whenever it happens, I spend countless hours reliving that look in my Daddy's eyes".

There's an unseen force squeezing the life out of Reece, ironically when he is in his most intensely human condition. He's struggling, but the pain is overtaking him. He blurts out, "I'm so sorry I killed those people. I didn't even think about their own family, but if I did, I wouldn't o' done it!" Reece is overcome by remorse and grief. There is nothing I can do. He knows it. I walk away.

ENDNOTES

[1]   In 1997, McCotter resigned his post with Utah's corrections system when a 29-year old schizophrenic prisoner died after being strapped naked to a restraint chair for 16 hours. In 2003, Attorney General John Ashcroft sent McCotter to Iraq to formulate a long term plan for Iraqi prisons, including Abu Ghraib.

ABOUT THE AUTHOR

Christopher Best is serving time at the Polunsky Unit in Livingston Texas. "LIVE! From Texas Death Row" won the PEN American Center's first prize for nonfiction in 2005. It was his first serious attempt at writing.

Contraband
Patricia Prewitt

Our digital clocks are now contraband. But if your old digital clock has a radio in it, then it's not contraband. The new replacement clocks the canteen now sells are digital. But they don't feature radios. Makes no sense? That's the point.

Of course, all the clocks to which I refer were or are sold in the prison canteen. So we purchase things then are told to get rid of these things and buy other things that are suspiciously like the very things we were forced to discard. This happens all the time.

Body powder, like Shower to Shower, is now contraband, but baby powder is not. Colored pencils bought in the canteen are contraband, but colored pencils bought through a craft order are not. Same pencils. Same brand. But not the same in the eyes of the powers-that-be. Better keep your receipt. Contraband items are still sold at the canteen. A lady who lives down my hall bought a headphone extension cord on Monday and was ordered to discard it on Wednesday.

Rumor has it that we will soon have to send out all our red or blue clothing because those are gang-related colors. I'm sitting here in a red turtleneck pullover. You know the kind. All middle-aged women have one. It's a classic style, comfortable, wears well, serves for a host of occasions – and I guarantee, I do not look like any kind of gang member. Unless we're referring to the over-the-hill gang. But if the scuttlebutt is true, I will be forced to get rid of this and pay for a new one in a less dangerous color – like green. But is Greenpeace considered a gang? What color is safe? If you wear pink or baby blue, could it mean you've pledged a gang but aren't a full member yet? Does purple signify you're straddling the fence?

In the mid '90s we had to get rid of all our black clothing because it was feared we would dress in black and pass for officers. Even black yarn became contraband, just in case we decide to crochet a baggy uniform. The E-Squad, a.k.a. Goon Squad, wears all black when they kick in on us for a shakedown.

Around that same time, we had to get rid of denim trousers and shorts. No reason was given for that decision. We can still possess denim shirts and jackets…just no denim below the waist. I remember in 1990 when we could still wear jeans, the rule was the jeans had to be dark indigo, not stonewashed, not acid-washed, no colors. The policy stated "blue jeans", and that description was taken quite literally.

It took some tall talking to explain that my indigo 501s could not sustain that dark color through repeated washings. An officer accused me of owning a pair of the dreaded contraband stonewashed jeans – when in truth, the poor Levis had started life dark blue but were just old and faded. I can relate.

Over many years of incarceration, I have spent a small fortune – remember that fortunes are relative – on items that were legal, only to find that they have been declared illegal. I have bought scissors, mirrors, tweezers, toenail clippers, Vicks VapoRub, can openers, highlighters, bed comforters, sheets, extension cords, stingers, crockpots, art and craft supplies, crochet hooks, reading lamps, clocks, oatmeal and honey facial scrub, key rings, dental floss, and more, in good faith only to find out I was holding contraband and could get in big trouble. Having purchased items through the proper channels is no defense in prison.

Most people think of prison contraband in terms of weapons or drugs – homemade knives, guns, and other harmful things. In our prison, contraband can be an extra pair of panties. We are allowed only seven. Guards frisk us in search of hard candy. A peppermint is contraband if found in a pocket.

I could write a book about prison contraband and never once mention a shank or tattoo gun – mainly because I've never even seen either in person. Only in movies. Come to think of it, I've never watched a prison movie where the convict was warned that his oatmeal and honey facial scrub had better be disposed of... or else.

Yesterday certain hours were set aside for us hapless prisoners to go to the Property Department to dispose of contraband. A huge line quickly formed of law-abiding ladies clutching body powder, digital clocks, colored pencils, and other questionable, although canteen-purchased items. An officer ordered all but five to return to their housing units, "There can only be five in the line at one time".

So the mob dispersed and trudged back. Once on the wing, this announcement was heard over the loud speaker, "Anyone wanting to send out contraband is to report to Property immediately!" Everyone gathered up her odds and ends and headed back to Property.

Once reassembled, the same officer again advised them of the five-in-the-line rule, so grudgingly they grumbled their way back to their quarters still in possession of the newly deemed contraband – only upon arrival to hear, "Last chance to send out contraband. Report to Property now!"

Handmade items are also problems. We are allowed one completed craft item and one in-progress craft item. In other words, I can have my completed afghan plus I can have one project on which I currently work. But as soon as I finish the last stitch on a crocheted teddy bear and clip the yarn, the innocent bear changes from "in-progress" to "completed" in a split second. Bam! Just that quickly I am in possession of one more completed craft item than I am allowed. One minute, I'm lawful. The next minute, I'm just begging for a contraband ticket. When we first arrived here at the new prison, cigarette lighters were contraband. Of course, no one is supposed to smoke in the buildings, so when smoke breaks were called the women had to beg lights from the officers outside the doors. In-wall lighters had been installed in the siding of the buildings, but these cheap appliances had ceased to function almost immediately.

Smokers, as all addicts, are ingenious and driven. The girls were actually rigging the inside electrical outlets to light their own cigarettes. Scary. Those with the proper skills traded sexual favors for lighters. The administration considered their options and relented. The girls can now buy lighters at the canteen.

Not only are certain items contraband, but where we put our stuff can make the stuff contraband. For instance, if I place my Bible on my locker, the Good Book becomes contraband. An innocent wet towel turns into contraband if draped over the locker door to dry. We are constantly on guard – ignore the pun – for infractions that so naturally occur when a person inhabits a space.

The inclination to set a plastic cup of instant coffee and a handful of chips on the locker near my bunk while I read a book is only natural. But if I let my guard down –there's that pun again – I can be in violation of the housing unit rule: "Two picture frames, one radio, and one locker scarf only allowed on top of the standing locker".

Even this rambling essay may very well be considered contraband. One of the definitions of the word contraband in our rule book states that it is anything that threatens the safety and security of the institution. Gosh. Maybe I should discard this.

ABOUT THE AUTHOR

After rejecting plea bargain offers, *Patricia Prewitt* was convicted and sentenced to Life With No Parole for 50 years for the 1984 murder of her husband. She and her children insist on her innocence. Now in her 60's with ten grandchildren, she is about halfway through the mandatory minimum of her sentence. She is housed at the Women's Eastern Reception, Diagnostic, and Correctional Center in Vandalia, Missouri, where she writes software and is one of only a handful of female prisoners who has earned Aerobics and Fitness Association of America certification as Personal Fitness Trainer, Griyp Exercise Instructor, and Step Aerobics. Through Prison Performing Arts program, she has performed as Lady Macbeth, Malvolio, and Bottom. "Contraband" took the PEN AMerican Center's first prize for nonfiction in 2006. Her poems are posted on her Facebook page. For an interview with her see http://www.pen.org/viewmedia.php/prmMID/1789/prmID/1644.

Fighting The Ninja
Charles Norman

Prison showers can be scary places. I'm not talking about those old "B" movie scenes where the big hairy guy with a handmade blade shanks the hapless prisoner for refusing to star in a gang rape, grimaces of pain, blood swirling down the drain, last words of "I love you, Mama", before the poor guy curls up and dies on the tiles.

Nowadays the showers are scary not from knives but from germs, leftovers from consensual acts clogging the pipes and floating sudsy sewage out into the hallways, catching those strolling unaware in flip-flops on a slippery stretch, skidding and cartwheeling, splashing onto their backsides into the mire.

I've spent my life in prison, and I'm not germaphobic by any stretch. Hell, I eat chow off those greasy, plastic trays every day, but at least they run them through hot water in some semblance of sanitation. Every day someone asks me for a cigarette. I tell them I don't smoke, I'm trying to get out of this prison alive, and lung cancer's not part of my plan. Neither is catching some creeping crud from the drain monster.

When I first came to prison the older men would joke that there was so much spilled seed from self-abuse in the shower that if you listened carefully you could hear millions of little voices down in the drain crying, "Daddy, Daddy".

I'd work out in the morning, come in to take a shower down the hall from my cell before lunch, and get grossed out by all the hair, melted soap, and gunk clogging the drains, the mold on the tiles, the musky odors, the scary streak running down the walls, the thoughts of what had gone on in there the previous evening to leave all that refuse behind. "Housemen" are those assigned to clean up every day, but the operative term has always been "sorry housemen", who shirked their duties, slept instead, and left the shower to molder, fester, and seethe.

I couldn't stand it anymore, so I asked the sergeant if he'd issue me the cleaning supplies and let me take care of that one shower. Incentive is virtually extinct in prison. His brow furrowed and his eyes darted around for thirty seconds or so, but he couldn't fathom any ulterior angle on my part, so he said okay.

It was hot. I'd lift some weights, jump some rope, get sweaty, check out a quart spray bottle of bleach, disinfectant, a scrub broom, cleaning rags, and a mop from supply, and head to the shower, a cell-sized room with three shower heads and a plastic curtain. I'd run the hot water for a few minutes, steaming things up, and then spray bleach from the ceiling to the floor, hitting the walls, drains, and curtain. I'd be in my workout shorts, walk away for ten minutes, let the bleach work and sterilize all the little organisms.

I'd come back and scrub every surface with the broom and disinfectant, run the hot water, clean all the hair and gunk out of the drains with rubber gloves on, wipe down and polish the walls and fixtures, then get my soap, shampoo, and towel, and take a cold shower with peace of mind, a rare commodity in prison. My shower was so clean that men from other wings and floors would line up to use it. Sometimes you become a victim of your own success. More usage meant more crud to clean up. It was a worthy investment nonetheless.

The sergeant was making his rounds one morning with his personal flunky, a notorious snitch and sycophant, a slightly-built white homosexual who personally screwed every sodomite who sought his favors. I was standing outside the shower spraying bleach, the chlorine fumes almost choking.

"Damn, Norman", he said, "That shit's strong. Why you spraying so much in that shower?" His little buddy, Brian, wrinkled his face and sneered at me, picking up his boss' cues that I might be chewed out momentarily.

I'd been lying in wait for someone official to ask me that very question. I pounced. "Well, Sarge, it's like this. Two fellas go in the shower and turn the water on real high. They soap each other up, and the big guy bends over the little guy, and shoves his thang way up in there, ripping and tearing loose the sewer lines. They'll be in here screeching like alley cats for awhile. Maybe the big guy knows it, maybe he doesn't care, but in amongst all that blood and shit and jism running down that boy's legs onto the floor are millions of little HIV viruses, several strains of hepatitis, maybe a couple shots of syphilis, gonorrhea, and herpes, and who knows what other contagious, and fatal diseases in a soupy stew".

"That's gross, Norman", Brian whines.

"Shut up", I snap. "You're the one I'm talking about".

The sarge is looking a little pale. Several synapses are crackling as he processes the images I'm painting in his head. I continue.

"Clots of all that stuff that spurted out of his diseased backside are simmering on the floor in pools. They dry off and leave. I come in, track through their remains, turn on the water, the stuff splashes over my feet and legs, and who knows, maybe I've got a fresh cut on my toe, and millions of little disease organisms leap and dive into that virgin bloodstream".

I take a breath. "That's one scenario. Or I can come in here with pure bleach, one of the few substances besides Lysol and nuclear radiation that will kill all that stuff, spray the place down real good, scrub every surface, rinse it off, and have a safe, sanitary shower for all of us".

"You're doing a good job", he says. "Keep it up". He hurries down the hall, his lapdog racing to catch up. We don't have to worry about the sergeant using our showers, I don't think.

Brian got sick and went into the infirmary for a couple of days. He came back out. He wasn't looking very healthy. He went back inside again. John, the orderly, confided that Brian was bleeding from the rectum, that the doctor had to pack his rear end with industrial-strength tampons, that his intestines had been ripped and torn so much it appeared someone had stuck a baseball bat in there. Days later they brought in a meat wagon. That's what they call an ambulance in prison. Usually when one of those comes for you, you're just a hunk of meat, not a person. It looked like one of those nature films, a crowd of prisoners watching the action in front of the clinic like a tightly-compressed herd of antelope staring at the lions devouring one of their less-swift relatives, each one thinking, better him than me.

The paramedics went inside wearing biohazard suits with the visors, like the ones in those Robin Cook disaster movies, pushing a stretcher with a plastic hood over it. They came back out with Brian strapped down and stretched out inside like the bubble boy, shoved him into the back of the meat wagon, and drove off. We didn't see him again. All quiet on the prison front. Something was seriously wrong with Brian, and it wasn't kidney stones, which is what the nurse told people.

In prison, they call HIV and AIDS, "the ninja", the black-clothed assassin that creeps inside and cuts your throat in the night, then slips away unseen, leaving you there to bleed out, alone.

There are certain disadvantages and responsibilities to being one of the few people in the prison with a formal education. In the kingdom of the dumb, the "Jeopardy!" champ isn't king, but some think he's the answer man, their personal source for every doubt and question.

It started the next day. Some of these big muscle-bound dudes become meek and fearful when they are confronted by things they can't pigeon-hole or find a place for in their tiny universe of understanding. I'd seen Roscoe accompanying Brian into the shower more than once, but his question caught me off guard.

"Norman, you're pretty smart". He wouldn't meet my eye, talking to the floor. "You heard about that boy Brian. They say he got that ninja".

"Yeah, Roscoe, I heard that".

"You know I was knockin' that boy off, right?", he asked.

"I kinda got that impression, Roscoe, but I try not to see certain things".

"I know you're not that way, Norman, you're not in the game, but I need to know something, and I respect your intelligence. You a straight dude, and you ain't gonna go repeating anything".

"I appreciate that Roscoe. What do you need to know?" He was having a hard time getting it out.

"Brian got that ninja. He dyin'. I was hitting him pretty regular. What do you think the chances are that I mighta' caught it from him?"

I frowned and shook my head. "That's a hard question to answer, Roscoe. Were you using any kind of protection?"

"Protection?" The big man tilted back his head and laughed. "Nah, we ain't never used no protection. Too late for that now. They don't sell rubbers in the canteen noways".

"I don't know what to tell you, Roscoe, except to go to medical and ask them to give you a test".

"They'll do that?"

"You have to ask".

"Thanks, man". He grasped both my hands in his big paws and squeezed, then hurried off, presumably to the clinic. I hoped for the best for him.

The next day Bible Willie came to my cell. He got his name because he carried an oversized Bible everywhere he went, to the chow hall, to work, to the softball field.

"I needs to talk with you, brother", he whispered, looking around. No one was near.

"You knows I's a Christian, right?", he said, holding up his ever-present Bible for emphasis.

I nodded. He had something to say. No sense interrupting his train of thought.

He took a deep breath. "I ain't always been a Christian, though".

"No?"

"No. A couple years ago I backslid for a spell. I was tempted, and I fell. I had sex with that boy Brian for a couple months".

"No shit!" I was surprised. It was like hearing that Jerry Falwell or Jim Bakker had succumbed to the flesh. Well, maybe not that bad.

"They say that boy got the ninja".

"Yeah", I heard."

"Tell me the truth". Willie pronounced it "troot". "You think I could have that ninja?"

"You're a Christian, right?", I asked.

"I'm a Christian".

"Then I suggest you pray, Willie".

"Will you pray with me?"

"I'd be proud to". We did. I felt a little weird at first, praying with this man who had fallen hard and risen and would probably fall again, but was scared now, and knew only to turn to his God for hope and comfort. But if you can't pray for a person like that, under such strange circumstances, how can you pray at all?

I suggested he get tested. He left, another satisfied customer.

Mama Herc was next. Mama Herc was a genuine prison legend, infamous beyond his razorwire boundary. When I was in the county jail for a couple of years fighting my case through the courts, recidivists shared chain gang horror stories about what would happen to the scared newcocks upon their arrival in prison. All that was missing in those jail cells to make it any scarier was crackling campfires and hooting owls.

"When you get to prison, boys," one scrawny, toothless thirty-year old six-time loser, with toothpick arms stained blue with crude self-inflicted tattoos crisscrossed with white razor blade scars, intoned, "You're gonna run into Mama Herc". He smiled, revealing gums, and smacked his lips.

"Who's Mama Herc?", some frightened teen burglar or car thief would always ask.

"Boy, Mama Herc is a sweet young white boy's worst nightmare", he'd say, warming up. "She, or he, whatever you wanna call it, is the biggest, meanest, strongest damn queer in the prison system. He's a monster, can lift all the iron in the weight pile, gets his strength and his protein from eatin' up young boys like you, and you, and you, every day".

"What?"

"Yep. Mama Herc's a black giant with plucked eyebrows and shaved legs, arms pumped up like Virginia hams. When I came into prison, sweet sixteen, all clean, not like I am now, I heard these footsteps behind me, turned around, and there was Mama Herc, the black Goliath, Frankenstein, Sasquatch, and Medusa rolled into one".

"What happened?"

"Mama Herc grabbed me by the throat with one hand, picked me up in the air, pulled me toward him, kissed me right dead on the lips, and grinned at me".

Groans and yechs resound.

"You should have smelled that breath. It'd make a vulture puke. Least he didn't stick his tongue in my mouth".

More groans and gags.

"Mama Herc looked me right in the eye and said, "White boy, I'm gonna suck your dick". And he did. What was I supposed to do?"

"When he got done, he squeezed my neck a little bit, just to let me know he could pinch off my head if he wanted to, and told me, "Now you're gonna suck mine"."

Louder gasps and groans.

"Mama Herc's still up there waiting for you boys to show up. When the bus pulls in, he'll be standing on the side with the others picking out the fish and the fresh meat. Welcome to prison".

Untold thousands heard those apocryphal tales of impending doom at the hands of Mama Herc, but the reality was quite different.

I'd been in jail for so long, had been in so many knockdown dragout fights over food trays, the TV or telephone, that I'd developed a reputation as "standup", one of the most revered praises, meaning that I wasn't afraid, would fight, wouldn't snitch. In prison your reputation precedes you, follows you, and often haunts you in a primal, often Biblical manner. Heaven help the cowardly, ratting child molester who exists at the very bottom of the pecking order and food chain.

So many murderers, robbers, kidnappers and thieves had passed through the county jail and made my acquaintance before they matriculated to the big house that when I finally got off the bus at Raiford, I was greeted by so many hardened convicts that you'd think it was a bizarre high school reunion.

Fellow standup convicts issued me the requisite razorsharp shank, a wicked, carbon steel prison knife made in the furniture factory, and clued me in on watching my back and avoiding homosexuals in the shower. Take showers in shifts. Wait till the "others" get out, go in with your homeboys, always have a few friends outside smoking cigarettes and standing guard.

I had a fresh life sentence, had lost my girl, been framed by crooked cops, and faced a long stretch ahead of me in prison with little chance of survival. I was not a happy camper. Early Saturday morning some of the boys came and got me, invited me to go to the weight pile and partake of some tomato puree buck, prison wine that packed a mule kick I didn't even know you could make wine out of tomato puree. I'm not a drinker, but it was early in my career, I was being tested, I wanted to be sociable, so I agreed to have one drink. Famous last words.

The guards didn't go around the weight pile. Too many steel bars and muscle men. It was early yet, 8 a.m., and besides my four friends and their three gallons of buck in bleach jugs, only one hardcore weight lifter made use of the facilities, a very large muscular black dude doing dead lifts with about six hundred pounds on a bar that bowed in the middle every time he lifted it.

I'm sure there's a drink that tastes worse than tomato puree buck, but I hope I never experience it. Prison alcoholics must have a masochistic streak to subject themselves to such punishment. It did its job, though. One cup turned into two, and suddenly I felt dizzy and lightheaded. Everyone was talking loud and laughing. I forgot about my plight and predicament, which was the point, I suppose. I got loud, too, and exceedingly irritated at the weight lifter who kept cutting his eyes back toward us, seemingly upset that several drunks were disturbing the tranquility of his weight pile so early in the morning.

He had a headband on, and several strands of those cheap pirate beads encircled his bull neck. When he dropped the weights with a clang and turned to stare at us, I noticed that his eyebrows were shaved and thin lines had been drawn on his forehead like a surprised clown. For some reason his disdainful look infuriated me, and the action of the tomato puree wine on my brain cells emboldened my normally taciturn temper.

"What you looking at?", I yelled.

His eyes narrowed, and he pointed his thumb at his chest, questioning.

"Yeah, you, you big musclebound motherfucker". His eyes widened. He wasn't used to being talked to like that. My friends shut up. He took a deep breath and stepped forward. I took two steps toward him. The alcohol had taken over my tongue.

"You want some of this, you overgrown piece of shit?" I shouted, hitting my chest with my fist. "Come on". I took another step. He took two.

"That's it. Come on, cocksucker", I bellowed. "I'll kick your fucking ass". I squared off in a karate stance.

"I'm not scared of those muscles. Bring it on. The first thing I'm gonna do is snap that fuckin' leg at the knee, then I'm gonna snap the other one, then the party begins".

He'd never said a word, but his eyes lasered fury and anger into me. He stopped. He breathed in and out several times, turned around, seized the steel bar loaded with weights, screamed, and flung the massive barbell into the air over his head. Then he threw the weights to the floor, chips of broken concrete flying everywhere with the clang of iron bouncing away as he stormed out of the weight pile. I flashed back to the original "King Kong" movie, when Kong was pulling up trees and slinging dinosaurs. We watched him hulk down the road. My buddy whistled.

"Man, do you know who that is?", one friend asked, looking at me strangely.

"I don't know and I don't give a fuck", I said, the wine still talking.

"That was Mama Herc", another said. "Man, if that cat got ahold of you he'd rip your arms off, he's so bad".

"I can't tell", I said. "He hauled ass".

"Yeah, he did". We went back to finish the dregs of tomato puree buck. The next day I awoke feeling like someone had drilled a two-inch hole through my skull. That was my first and last foray into buck territory.

A week later, I was in the chow line with Murf the Surf, another chain gang legend who'd become infamous for stealing jewelry from a New York museum, but was serving life for the murders of a couple of women in South Florida. Murf was like the prison welcome wagon, taking promising new prisoners in hand and introducing them to prison society.

They were serving fried chicken and the chow hall was crowded. Murt made his way toward the back where a huge black man sat at a table alone, hunkered over a tray, tearing into a large chicken breast like a starving dog. Mama Herc. Uh oh. Nothing good could come of this. Murf greeted Herc like a long-lost brother, and motioned if we could sit down. Herc nodded, not missing a bite of the greasy chicken. Herc's eyes never left mine.

"Herc, I want you to meet a good friend of mine, Charlie. Charlie, Herc".

Herc took a breath. "We met", then resumed crunching up the chicken bones.

That threw Murf off for a second, wondering how we'd met, and him not knowing about it.

For all his size Mama Herc actually had a soft voice that belied his reputation as a maneater. I'd never actually heard a sound out of him besides a scream and bellow.

"Murf", he said, wiping his mouth. He pronounced it, "Moif". He cut his eyes to me. "He's yo' frien'?", he asked.

Murf nodded, amused, sensing something.

"Dat cat's one crazy cracker", he said, spooning mashed potatoes and gravy into his cavernous mouth.

Murf grinned. "Why do you say that, Herc?"

"Last week I was workin' out, and that cat called me every kind of motherfucker and cocksucker they is".

"No shit!" Murf was astounded. "What happened?"

"I was gonna try him, but he said he was gonna break both my legs, and then really fuck me up. The way he looked, I thought he might be able to do it, so I just said fuck it and went to my cell".

Murf looked at me. My turn.

I acknowledged that it had happened.

"I owe you an apology", I said. "I didn't even know who you were. I had a couple cups of that tomato puree buck those guys in the kitchen made, and it went to my head. I never should have said those things. Will you accept my apology?" I extended my hand across the table. The moment of truth. If he wanted to do something here, I was in trouble.

He reached across and my hand disappeared into his. He shook it. I tried to shake back, but I could feel the bones in my hand crackling. He wasn't even squeezing hard. I hoped he'd turn it loose. He did.

"We straight", he said, meaning no hard feelings, and resumed scouring his tray.

Months later Herc signed up for a prisoner self-help program where men spend days sitting in a circle and telling their life stories, among other activities. Herc opened up, and I learned the terrible truth behind his chain gang legend.

He'd gone to the state reform school not much more than a scrawny child, and had been brutally raped, abused, and passed around by the older teens. He was too small to fight them off. His life was a living hell for weeks and months. He turned to the weight pile, desperate to add size and become strong, and in a couple years, he'd spurted upward, at fifteen, bigger and stronger than most fully-grown men. By then he'd developed a taste for homosexuality, and the weak prey of years past morphed into a predator.

Now he was a grown man, having spent most of his life in captivity, turning into that which he'd feared and hated most as a helpless youth. He denied the veracity of the chain gang stories about his attacking fresh young prisoners in years past, and beneath that frightening exterior a little boy still hid.

I developed a respect for Herc, for his sheer determination as a survivor. I'd been a grown man when I came to prison. I couldn't imagine how damaging and horrifying it might have been had I come to prison as a child. Might I have developed into something like Mama Herc? I shuddered to think about it. I would rather have died. Many did.

We became friends, as odd as that may seem. He had a child-like innocence of many things. He'd never had a life in society, never had a job, never drove a car. He was scared to death of women. He was insecure and uneducated, and had no skills but one. He was the strongest man in prison. He owned the weight pile. He was truly institutionalized, a product of his environment, and life in a "free society" was as alien to him as life on Mars or Jupiter.

Years passed. Anytime there was a dispute of a fact Mama Herc would bring the arguing parties to me. "Now ask Norman. He knows everything". Not quite, but more than most of them. Whatever I said they accepted. So when Mama Herc came to me about the ninja and that boy, Brian, I felt very sad. What could I say?

"You know what I wanna ask you about?" He pronounced ask, "axe".

I nodded. "Brian".

"Yeah, that boy. You know I had a thing about that boy for awhile".

"I didn't know that, Herc, but I'm not surprised".

"He was fine at one time, before he got sick".

I said nothing.

"They say that boy got the ninja. That's some bad shit. What you think, Norman? You think I got it, or mighta' got away with it?"

"I don't know, Herc. It's hard to say without a blood test".

"I don't want no blood test. You know I'm scared of needles".

"It depends, Herc, on the risky behavior", I said. "If you were pitching and he was catching, and he had it, the odds are a lot better than if the roles were reversed, if he were pitching and you were catching".

Herc dropped his head, then looked at me. He shook his head, resigned.

"We was playing all positions, my man, back and forth".

I couldn't say anything. I put my hand on his shoulder as scant comfort, one friend to another, and the big man began crying, whether for himself or the lost boy, I did not presume to know.

He leaned down to my shoulder and sobbed, shaking. I couldn't reach around him, he was too big, but at least I could reach to his back and pat him as my grandmother had done me when I was a little boy, hurt, crying from a stubbed toe. We were standing in the hallway in front of my cell. Men passed by, staring, then averting their eyes at the incongruous scene, the massive black homosexual crying on the shoulder of the straight white dude comforting him. Nobody said a word. Nobody dared.

When I didn't think it could get any worse, an hour later Pop Blakely came to my cell. I was trying to write a letter.

Pop Blakely was a scrawny, wizened black man in his seventies, perpetually hacking and coughing, his lungs seizing up, a cigarette always stuck between his lips and a cup of coffee in one hand. He didn't weigh one hundred pounds, and looked like he'd died a couple years before but had forgotten to lie down and be still. He coughed for a full minute, took a sip of his coffee and hit off the cigarette, and spoke.

"Norman, you know that boy Brian was in my cell the past six months, right?"

I snapped. "Jesus Christ, Pop, not you too! Am I the only person in this prison who hasn't screwed that boy!"

"You might be". He hacked and wheezed some more until I thought chunks of his lungs might come out, but instead he spit a thick yellow gob of mucous into my toilet and flushed it.

"They put the boy in the top bunk of my cell", he said. He took another puff and blew the smoke out into the hallway out of deference to my not smoking.

"I was laying there playing with myself", he continued. "I had the old snake out, and I was trying to slap some life into it".

I tried to banish the images from my mind to no avail.

"That boy, Brian, heard me down there, and he popped his head over the side of the bunk, looked at me, and said, "Pop, you ain't gotta' do that, let me do it for you", so I told him like that guy on TV said, come on down!"

We both burst out laughing. I couldn't help it. Pop Blakely went off on a coughing jag, spat, wiped his rheumy eyes, then spoke again.

"What you think the odds are that I got that ninja from that boy?"

"How old are you, Pop, seventy-five?"

"Seventy-two".

"I hear you got diabetes, a bad heart, lung cancer, and tuberculosis".

"Don't forget the emphysema and the kidneys", he added.

"You smoke how many packs of cigarettes a day?"

"I cut down to two packs of ready-rolls a day".

"Pop, with all that wrong with you, I wouldn't worry about the ninja". He seemed satisfied with that answer, and scuttled away.

Time went by. Brian's gone. Roscoe's gone. Bible Willie's gone. Mama Herc's gone. Pop Blakely is long gone. I'm still here.

I watched those poor people in New Orleans after Katrina hit, wading chest-deep and neck-deep through toxic flood waters, pushing their meager belongings in a garbage bag ahead of them, pushing their grandma on a mattress, dead animals floating by, the city turned into a massive sewer.

Prison is also a sewer. To survive prison you must wade carefully through the sewage, sometimes it's waist-deep, sometimes it's neck-deep, sometimes it's over your head. You have to slowly navigate through the rats and vermin and turds swimming and floating along with you. You are immersed in it, but if you're determined you can keep your mouth and nose and eyes above it, don't let it get inside you, bide your time, and when you get to the other side you can cast off your filthy clothes, wash and clean and dry yourself, and leave the stink of the prison sewer behind.

Some don't. Some dive headfirst into the waters of the prison sewer, they inhale deeply, take it all in, become a part of it. And they die. Some live, but are irrevocably changed.

As for myself, I stand in front of my shower with my spray bottle filled with bleach, making sure I cover the walls and floor and especially the drains, serving my life sentence, wondering if I will ever go home.

* "Mama Herc", photo by Charles Norman (1985).[1]

ENDNOTES

[1] I took the photo shortly before Mama Herc's release from prison. I was in charge of the "Jaycee Photo Project" at Zephryhills Correctional Institution, and took 35 mm photos on weekends for $1.50, two copies. Herc was getting out soon, and I told him, "Why don't I take a photo, Herc? After you're gone, people won't know what you really looked like". He said he'd like to, but he had no money. I agreed to pay for the photo, give him one copy and keep the other for the "historical record". It was a real scene, Herc's photo. Must have been a hundred prisoners watching out of camera range. Herc was very nervous. The last photo taken of him had been the one taken at the Lake Butler prison reception center so many years before, the day he came to prison. He adjusted his "doo rag" and his beads, finally just flexed his muscles and I snapped the photo. He was so proud of it, and I'm so glad I took it. When I first met Mama Herc at Raiford in 1980, the original setting for "Fighting The Ninja", he was perhaps 40 pounds heavier and solid muscle. In between 1980 and 1985, Herc spent 18 months at the Brooksville Road Prison working from daylight to dark on the road crews which burned him down to 240 pounds or so – a shadow of his former self. He was still incredibly strong. Mama Herc was released shortly after the photo was taken and went to St. Petersburg , Florida. The 'prison grapevine' reported that he didn't last long on the outside and was killed within a year or so of release. Mama Herc, whose real name was Alphonia Smith, a true chain gang legend, lives on in countless apocryphal stories of his prison exploits.

ABOUT THE AUTHOR

Charles Norman has been in Florida prisons for more than 30 years. His poems, short stories, essays and memoirs have received numerous national writing awards ever since he won awards from Mensa and PEN in 1986.

In 2009, he won the Outstanding Achievement Award, given infrequently by the PWP. "Fighting the Ninja" took first place in the memoir category in 2008. He continues his fight for freedom in a high-tech world that has changed greatly, writing a blog (see http://charlienorman.blogspot.com), embracing Facebook, and sending emails and communiqués from prison. Friends maintain his website, www.freecharlienow.com.

Rage, Criminal Justice, and Corrections
William Steed Kelley

A walloping THUMP startled me. It felt like a sledge hammer crashing against the wall – my bunk was bolted to. I fumbled my book and leapt to my feet, my heart racing and pounding in my throat.

"You ready to rock?", a deep voice rumbled.

I grabbed my shaving mirror and poked it through the front of my cell, making eye contact with Hitman – the massive, muscular, and certifiably mad East Texas Good Ol' Boy in the next cell.

"You asked me to hang onto your radio. You didn't say anything about having to rock and roll!", Hitman laughed.

The Aryan Brotherhood (AB) was out three hundred dollars and half an ounce of weed on his watch. By the law of the jungle, Hitman had to produce either the money, or the blood – and blood came much easier to him than money, especially these days. He'd just the week before gotten a Dear John letter from his gorgeous wife – a blond Redneck Girl – who strongly resembled Lorrie Morgan, the country and western singer. We all knew Hitman would go berserk, we just didn't know when.

On Friday, a black Special Operations Response Team guard named Fontenot had "jacked" the AB's mule for his pack and given it to the Building Tender – a "trustee" who happened to be "MW", a Mandingo Warrior. When their shift reported for duty again the next rotation, Hitman and The Brotherhood were ready for them. Hitman had gotten his hands on some weaponry – a mop and long-handled, wooden "shitter brush" – fished from the nearby mop closet with a weighted strip of bedsheet.

"He's passin' out shitpaper – headed this way. I'm fixin' to gig the shit outta this fuckin' toad", he said, glee ringing in his voice.

When the Building Tender – called a "BT" – had feigned ignorance to the whereabouts of the AB's contraband, Hitman had secretly unscrewed the mophead, straightened the three-sixteenths diameter retainer loop into a two-foot-long spear, sharpened the tip and lashed it to the mopstick. It was now an oversized frog-gig. The shitter brush he'd soaked in wet towels over the weekend – after tearing all the bristles out. That was the sledgehammer which had bowled me out of bed all the way through the four inch-thick concrete wall between us. It had an eighteen inch-long oak handle as thick as a closet pole and was now a war hammer worthy of Thor.

The BT working his way down the cellblock passing out toilet paper to us had made a terrible mistake in accepting Fontenot's gifts "compliments of the Aryan Brotherhood". And with his blatant favoritism toward black prisoners when it came to serving portions at meal times and quality of clothing necessities, the whites and Hispanics already resented him – Hitman especially so. Now he was about to pay the price.

My pulse quickened with his approach. He was alone, dragging a large box of toilet tissue, bending over and stuffing it into the low feeding chutes in our cell doors.

Warning him was out of the question. As a "Newboot" – and general prison survival policy – I wanted *no* part of this coming conflict. It was already bad enough that I'd been duped into holding Hitman's radio.

When he got to Hitman's cell, I watched in silence as he prattled inanities to someone on the tier above, heedless of the stone-cold killer lurking only a few feet away. When he bent to stuff a roll into Hitman's cell, there was a "Heeyah!" and the rattle of wooden mophandle against steel bars.

The spear shot out, went completely through his abdomen and out his back, then retracted with a grunt from both of them, and shot out once more to again impale him with another, "Heeyah!"

Blood speckled the back of his starched white uniform shirt, but curiously, none came out the front. I saw the shock in his eyes as his mind belatedly registered that he might already be dead.

He wheeled backward, turned, and ran to the crash gate, screaming in pain and terror. Blood – apparently coming from his anus – began to stain his inner thighs and buttocks quite heavily.

"He stabbed me!", he hollered. "He speared me!"

Hitman cackled as pandemonium broke wide throughout the cellblock. Guards yelled and barked orders. Heavy brass keys on thick rings jangled and rattled into locks. Steel doors slammed, the loud echoes reverberating everywhere. Finally, the electronically controlled crash-gate popped open with a loud clang and the BT scurried off to the infirmary, slumping to hold his guts.

"How you like that, nigger?", Hitman shouted after him. "I'll kill all you bitches! You Dingleberry Warriors suck my honky dick, howbout? Huh?", Hitman chortled, then tossed the spear out onto the catwalk, where it rattled in deadly commentary on his deed.

"You a ho-ass white boy!", someone shouted from the tier above. Others – black, white and Hispanic – joined in the verbal fracas of mutual hate and death threats.

I turned my mirror back around to look at Hitman. He was breathing hard, and smiling, eyes ablaze. He turned and busied himself with a blanket, erecting a blind in preparation for Phase Two.

A moment later, the shift supervisor – a muscular black guard named Hightower – strode onto the scene, cautiously approaching Hitman's cell. He kicked the spear farther away.

"What the fuck, Bonner?", he asked.

Hitman gave only a hearty, full-throated laugh.

"Take that blanket down, Bonner".

"Suck my cock—*Sarge* . . . "

Hightower looked as if he couldn't believe what he'd heard. "Oh yeah?", he said. "That blanket's *coming* down. You gonna cop that pussy, or fight my team, white boy?"

"I'm gonna *kill* your goddamn team".

Hightower shook his head. "No, we're gonna smash your stupid, peckerwood ass".

"That's Mr. Peckerwood to you, nigger". Again, Hitman's insane laugh.

Hightower's face was a violent storm. "Don't go anywhere, Bonner", he quipped, "'cause it's about to be Mr. Nigger, to you".

With that, Hightower laughed nervously and stalked off to suit up his react team.

Hitman disappeared behind his blanket, making last-minute arrangements. In preparation, he'd collected several weeks' worth of newspaper from others, crumpled the individual sheets, and doused the knee-high, wall-to-wall pile with two large bottles of baby oil. He'd also coated the floor with petroleum jelly and rigged a trip-line low on the cell entranceway.

He knocked the war club against my wall again as he climbed atop the upper bunk, gaining high-ground advantage.

Within a few minutes, the react team came stomping in formation through the crash gate, Fontenot – as expected – wielding the steel shield in front of them like a battering ram. A female video camera operator trailed several yards behind, taping the Use-of-Force extraction.

When they reached Hitman's cell, Fontenot slammed the shield against the front of it, employing the unnerving impact to full psychological effect. Startled yet again, my heart leaped back into my throat.

Hightower shouted, "Inmate Bonner, I'm giving you a direct order to submit to a strip-search and hand restraints".

"Suck it, niggerrr", Hitman drawled from behind his blind. He made loud meowing sounds and laughed at himself.

"The inmate has refused the first command", Hightower said, dictating into the record.

"Inmate Bonner, this is your second and final order to submit to a strip-search and hand restraints".

"Gonna kill you whore dogs . . . ", Hitman growled.

"At this time the inmate has refused my second command to submit to a strip-search and restraints. Force will be utilized to gain his compliance".

When they realized action was imminent, the prisoners in the cellblock began to chant and hoot, "HooHa! HooHa! HooHa!", banging in rhythm on their cell bars. Hightower now had to shout at the top of his lungs to be heard.

"Team, ready positions!"

Fear was evident in the wide-eyed looks of the five strong men – three black and two white – dressed in full riot gear. They shook as they bunched-up in close, single-file formation, their hands trembling on the shoulders of the one in front and Fontenot nervously throttling the steel handles of the battering shield.

"On my signal", Hightower shouted.

The cacophony in the cellblock redoubled. "Hoo! Hoo! Hoo!" Bang! Bang! Bang!"

The security pin popped from its slot with a loud clang in the gearworks of Hitman's cell door. The team shifted their feet, trying for better traction. Hightower lifted a hand into the air and circled it. "Roll it!", he shouted.

The cellblock exploded in cheers of bloodlust, the prisoners shouting and shaking their cell doors in proxy participation. The heavy door on Hitman's cell ground in complaint as it made its slow concourse.

"Yaaarghhh!", Hitman let fly a barbarian warcry from somewhere so deep within it made my hair stand on end. The team answered with their own cries, but I could sense fear in theirs. There was no fear in Hitman – none.

Just as suddenly, they rushed in, boots digging and stomping like a cattle stampede.

Boom! The very first crash was clearly Hitman's warclub against one of the retrofitted motorcycle helmets. It sounded like Barry Bonds smashing a coconut with his Louisville.

"Heeyah! Heeyah! Heeyah!" Each expulsion of effort was followed by a crushing, devastating blow from the club.

The battering shield smashed into the commode in the back of the cell, shattering it and sounding like an avalanche of boulders tumbling around inside a cement mixer.

Someone screamed, "Aaahhh! Fire! Fire!"

Hightower was outside his cell, hopping around on the balls of his feet, trying to get a view into the melee.

"Oh shit! Retreat! Retreat! Retreat!", he shouted. The flames were flaring up.

The team scrambled out, going backward faster than they had gone in, and Hitman chased them with his club, leaving Fontenot lying in the roiling fire, unconscious.

Hitman roared, swinging the club with both hands. To prevent from being disarmed, he had it lanyarded around his right wrist through a hole in the end of the handle.

The four remaining team members panicked, scattering in every direction. Hitman chased one and then the other here and there. When he went after Hightower, he too scrambled.

Hitman's eyes fell on the camera operator. He charged.

She didn't have the camera's safety strap around her neck, and when she realized her danger, dropped it with a scream and ran up the stairs.

Canned goods, cups, boots and light bulbs began raining down from the tiers above, pelting the guards and Hitman alike.

Hitman stopped when he got to the camera and stomped it to a million pieces, then turned to hunt the closest team member. He backed one into a corner and behind a fifty-five-gallon trash barrel. The guard tried to take cover using the lid as a shield, but one blow from the club knocked it away.

Hitman continued flailing at odd angles, but was unable to land any solid blows.

Hightower ran into the blazing cell and pulled Fontenot out by the boots. Blood streamed from his face where Hitman had knocked his face-shield away entirely.

With Fontenot out of the flames, Hightower rushed Hitman from behind, tackling him over the trash barrel. Together, they rolled to the right.

Hitman twisted around and overpowered Hightower, getting his right arm around his neck and pushing the handle of the club into this throat, choking him. He then bit a large chunk of Hightower's scalp and shook his head, growling like a pit bull and tearing the flesh away, drawing copious rivulets of blood. Hightower's eyes bugged and his mouth gaped in struggle for air that would not come.

With Hightower and Hitman grappling, the other team members returned to join the struggle. They eventually broke Hitman's grip on Hightower, permitting him – now gasping – to gain his feet. When he did get some air, he squared up and planted a devastating kick right to Hitman's face. The impact cracked audibly, and Hitman went limp.

They wrestled him facedown into the concrete and Hightower squared up again, landing another combat boot to his face. He then danced around into a new position and stomped on Hitman's right elbow. The bones cracked in report.

Hitman grunted in pain as Hightower knelt and helped twist the now useless arm. They slapped cuffs on his wrists and leg irons on his ankles. It was the last I saw of Hitman before they dragged him around the corner by his chains and resumed beating him – out of sight of any witnesses.

I shouted in disgust, "Stop it! He's restrained!"

Hightower came back around the corner, blood pouring from his head, to give me a "You're next" look. When the medics arrived, he helped carry Fontenot away on the gurney.

I looked at the streams of blood on the floor and saw two teeth lying there. The fire hose was quickly unrolled and the teeth washed away as the cell fire was extinguished.

* * *

I saw Hitman again, about ten years later and in another facility. He'd lost much of his mass and muscle tone, and his hair had for the most part fallen out. Where once there had been thick, brown hair, there was now a pattern of massive scarring. Hitman could not recall any of that day's horrors nor did he recognize me. I noticed changes in his mannerisms and bearing – he was getting an early start on his second childhood.

* * *

Texas, the "Lone Star", is unique in many ways. That makes its gully features uniquely horrendous. Texans take perverse pride in the exploits of Judge Roy Bean – a man with no allegiance to ideas of due process – and John Wesley Hardin – a notoriously mean, gunfighting serial killer.

Government officials would have us believe incidents like Hitman's are unavoidable in prison. But the little things, those which could have been addressed appropriately, leading up to such enraged attacks are never seen, seldom explained, rarely understood.

The Texas Department of *Corrections* has, since Hitman's day, changed its name to Department of Criminal Justice – Institutional Division, and stopped addressing us as "inmates"; now we're "offenders".

But it's the government that's on the offense. There remains no pretense to "corrections", and despite the insightful warnings of mental health and behavioral experts, from coast to coast hundreds of thousands of men and women just like Hitman are locked in cages, treated like animals, driven to frustrated, self-defeating rage, exploited in their downfall, and then unleashed upon an unsuspecting society to begin the cycle all over again.

These *fellow-citizens* who, for whatever reason, lack capacity for constructive problem-solving skills or the personal insight necessary to reconfigure self-defeating thought patterns, are being encouraged to act upon their frustrations with violence.

Each reported use of force or disciplinary infraction report – even threats to sue, which, in Orwellian Newspeak constitute a "verbal assault" – are reported to the legislature and contribute to increased funding for the prison.

A Texan on Death Row, perhaps in order to prove his insanity gouged out his own eyes and swallowed them. Others shred themselves with razorblades, overdose on drugs, and hang themselves.[1]

In Texas, prison guards who use force – allegedly in foiling an attempted escape, saving the life of another officer, or preventing a riot – are often commended, promoted in rank and pay grade, and might find themselves in *Correctional Peace Officers' Magazine,* named as Officer of the Month.

It will probably never be known how many little defeats Hitman suffered along the way to giving up altogether. But each little defeat of another person in this life is yet another defeat for all of us.

ENDNOTES

[1] The extent of the mutilation and the determination exhibited by prisoners to engage in serious acts of self-harm is astonishing. Prisoners have swallowed pins, inserted pencils in their penises and paperclips in their abdomens, bitten chunks of flesh from

their arms, slashed and gashed themselves. In many prisons around the country, Human Rights Watch has interviewed prisoners whose bodies are massively scarred from self-mutilation. Both correctional and mental health staff acknowledge that self-mutilation is a major problem. See "Suicide and Self-Mutilation" in *Ill-Equipped,* a Human *Rights Watch Report*, October 21, 2003.

ABOUT THE AUTHOR

Coffield Unit at the Tennessee Colony prison in Texas currently houses *William Steed Kelley.* "I was introduced to the endemic violence Texas chooses to call criminal justice just a few weeks after high school graduation", he writes. He is now 41. He took the Long Ridge Writers' Group writing course "to acquire the skills necessary to give appropriate expression to what I *must* say before departing this world. With time and practice I have found that writing helps me decide what I really think and feel about things – one has to understand before anyone else can be made to understand through writing". These 23 years can never be returned, he writes, "but my life – however difficult – *will* serve a positive purpose if I have to move heaven and earth to that end". This essay is his first publication. An earlier version, "The Seeds of Jasper Hate", won the PEN American Center's second prize for nonfiction in 2007.

Convicts and Communities
Jorge Antonio Renaud

Restoring dignity to convicts – which is a definition of rehabilitation – is not much in vogue in America. There is little demand for rebuilding broken individuals and reintegrating them into distrustful communities. Bickering between get-tough conservatives and give-love-a-chance liberals has squeezed most convict/citizen interaction into irrelevance, and pragmatic proposals are derided as a) too costly, b) posing security risks, or c) pandering to society's debris, a charge deadly to a budding politician's aspirations.

A few lonely programs exist. Other than faith-based, evangelical experiments, convict/citizen interaction can be clumped into three categories: prisoner trustees sent into communities to provide labor; prisoners invited to speak to youth organizations about the nexus of drugs and crime; and at-risk youth sent day-tripping into max institutions by judges held rapt by the "Scared Straight" mythos.

All three categories are exclusionary and non-representational. They limit participation to prisoners handpicked by prison officials. The first two groups in Texas are almost exclusively young, non-violent offenders with short sentences. Armed robbers, rapists and murderers are rarely granted trustee status and will not be fighting fires or building homes in local communities, and they surely won't be addressing the Boys and Girls Club. Any tangible benefits accruing from these programs are denied to all prisoners not allowed in.

The "Scared Straight" paradigm, along with the boot camp concept, has been mostly discredited. If fear and certain violence were true barriers to recidivism, one trip to prison would be more than enough to dissuade young men and women from further crime. This has never been so. "Scared Straight" programs make for good theater and little else. However much the tattooed, toothless terrors picked for these programs hew to traditional convict caricatures, they still are carefully screened by prison officials to fit certain criteria – here an external fierceness coupled with the ability to follow with a meaningful message.

The truth is, programs of this type aren't designed to inculcate responsibility in or enhance the rehabilitation of participating prisoners. They aim to provide prison officials a way to bond with community leaders, and to allow each group to then point to these cooperative efforts as examples of what "good inmates" can do, if only they are taken in hand and pointed in the right direction. The fact that "good" in this instance reflects certain prison officials' concept of trustworthiness is typical of current prison rehab programs – they are denied to the very prisoners whose history shows a desperate need of them.

Sincere programs committed to helping prisoners lift themselves from the despair of their existence, if inviting real and substantial community involvement, would have the following components:

1) They would be cheap, emphasizing volunteers and prisoner peer groups instead of paid prison employees. Politicians cannot resist ranting against prison programs that someone, somewhere, has insisted are a "luxury". College programs, writing workshops, arts and crafts, and legitimate recreational programs for elderly and handicapped prisoners have been cut in various prisons after citizen complaints. Much as they'd like, politicians can muster little argument against programs proposed, initiated and staffed by community volunteers or unpaid prisoners.

2) They would be as inclusive as possible and would in fact focus on the medium, close and high security prisoners that most prison programs now exclude. Texas, for example, offers adequate anger management, cognitive intervention and substance abuse programs. However, the very prisoners whose disciplinary records show violations reflecting poor thinking skills, anger problems or continued substance abuse are the only inmates excluded from those classes. Astonishingly, Texas demands that prisoners attain an arbitrary custody level and remain disciplinary-free for a set period – in other words, to show that they have on their own realized and begun to address their problems – before allowing them the "privilege" of entering programs that should have been mandated once their problems were discovered. It is this mindset, of allowing prisoners into programs based on false security criteria instead of demonstrable need that necessitates the following.

3) They would require volunteer professionals to conceive of and provide non-institutional models of cognitive thinking – ideally a Socratic approach to ethical problems – without the input or participation of prison officials or staff. Prison officials would of course retain the right to allow or deny a given program, but the goals, methods and all particulars of classroom or program essentials would be conceived of

and presented by volunteers or prisoners. Prison-initiated programs, and the state employees who staff them, are infused with the belief that all prisoners are game players, all saying and doing anything to get over and get out. This attitude is inescapable; it is gospel, taught at the guard academies. This not-so-subtle contempt taints what good these programs offer, and they offer quite a bit. A recent review of evidence-based programs for criminalized adults evaluated the results from 291 programs over the last 35 years. Programs emphasizing cognitive thinking consistently reduced recidivism rates by significant percentages, especially when coupled with community involvement (Aos et al., 2006).

4) Finally, these programs would demand that prisoners give to the community not what prison orders them to give, but what their skills and experience allows them to give, reinforcing the validity of those skills and experience.

So what would these programs – cheap, initiated within the community, focused on prisoners needing immediate help and accepting what they have to offer – actually look like?

They would flow in and out. An inflow program could be initiated by a local philosophy professor, an attorney or anyone with good verbal skills and knowledge of the Socratic teaching method. This approach demands that the student peel away layers of assumption and behavior until arriving at an underlying truth.

In this instance, volunteers could hold round-table discussions with close or medium custody prisoners, preferably in cell-block dayrooms to alleviate security concerns and to avoid taking classroom space. Volunteer moderators would post ethical conundrums relevant to prison life to the prisoners, asking them to explain their solutions.

This tactic is called playing The Whys, a game that author Ronald Gross (2002) credits cognitive anthropologist Charles Case with creating. It consists of asking someone "Why?" questions that elicit the reason or motivation for each preceding response. The answers may seem childish or robotic at first, but if honestly pursued they eventually reveal core values.

And the assumption of these round-table groups – or any of these cognitive thinking programs – is that all inmates retain core values, but their behavior has been twisted by the short-term rewards of situational ethics.

Using various cognitive thinking exercises – The Whys being only one – community volunteers use the moral goodness implicit in their altruism and willingness to enter prisons to strengthen prisoners' dormant sense of basic right and wrong. With the reinforcement of the group, prisoners *can* express their frustration with prison's rigid code. Surely, this is better than ordering prisoners to clean a trash-filled alleyway.

The success or failure of this program can be easily quantified. In a pilot program on one or two cell-blocks, disciplinary records of participating prisoners could be tracked and compared with disciplinary records of like-custody prisoners who did not take part. Prisoners completing these courses and moving into minimum custody could then hold round-tables of their own, equipped with necessary materials such as videos and books, with a moderator occasionally sitting in.

Outflow programs present more of an opportunity for extensive convict/ community interaction. Prisoners leaving still on paper (e.g. those on parole or some type of supervised discharge) would prepare a Personal Penance Statement, which would set out to the community and government agency overseeing release the manner in which that prisoner felt he or she could best contribute to the community.

While similar to existing programs that require community service, most of those not only *compel* that service; it is punitive, based on the negative reinforcement of humiliation. Personal Penance announces: This is who I am. This is what I can do to give back. By accepting, the community positively reinforces the prisoner/parolee's sense of worth.

For example, inmate mechanics could promise to donate one weekend a month to help repair cars of low-income families. Once released, they would register with an office at the parole agency. Community participants would by then have found a local auto shop owner willing to donate garage space and tools. One weekend a month, low-income car owners would be invited to bring their cars in – or to have them towed in – for repairs and would be charged only for parts, the labor being donated by the parolees.

Every outgoing inmate can be asked to provide a Personal Penance Statement. Every inmate has something he or she can offer – electricians, gardeners, carpenters, janitors, printers, sewing machine operators, clothes pressers – all can promise to use their skills to benefit those who need help, everything done for the community, in conjunction with community assistance.

Crucial to this is that those accepting work from the parolees be allowed to thank them personally. It would not do for a volunteer to be a cutout at the auto shop, allowing no interaction between the owners of the vehicles and the parolee mechanics. If any of these programs are to be of any use besides providing cheap labor, it is necessary that the community not be shielded from the prisoners/parolees, but that they are now integral, respected members of the community.

These are but two examples of possible ways to foster interaction and build trust between free citizens and those they have exiled. Obstacles to their implementation will be familiar: prison officials unwilling to allow outsiders into their fiefdoms; politicians barking that any program is wasted on human scum; and the deadening inertia that plagues any prison initiative suggesting something new. And of course, some prisoners will fail. Some will take advantage where they shouldn't. The naysayers will howl, "You see? They cannot be trusted!"

But the possibility for change is ever present. All we need to do is to believe, to truly believe that each man and woman is blessed with a kernel of redemption, and to then ask ourselves: do we nourish it, or do we let it wither and die?

REFERENCES

Aos, Steven, Marna Miller and Elizabeth Drake (2006) *Evidence-Based Adult Correction Programs: What Works and What Does Not?*, Olympia (WA): Washington State Institute for Public Policy.

Gross, Ronald (2002) *Socrates' Way: Seven Master Keys to Using your Mind to the Utmost*, New York: Jeremy Tarcher, pp. 31-32.

ABOUT THE AUTHOR

Jorge Antonio Renaud is the author of *Behind the Walls: A Guide for Families and Friends of Texas Prison Inmates*, published by the University of North Texas Press. He was a copy editor at the *Austin American-Statesman* and the *Waco Tribune-Herald.* The Houston Trial Lawyers Association awarded him the 2003 First Amendment Award for his defense of free speech while editor of the Texas prisons newspaper, *The Echo.* His short fiction, poems, memoirs, and essays have taken many prizes in the PEN Prison Writing Contest over the years. "Convicts and Communities" took third place in nonfiction in 2007. Now free, Jorge is involved with reentry initiatives in Texas, specifically working to develop and offer cognitive behavioral programs to all Texas convicts. He offers consultation services to anyone interested in Texas prisons through his website, exforgood.com.

No English, Gracias
Marilyn Buck

I teach English as a Second Language (ESL). As a poet and a writer, I recognize and believe in the power of the word, not only because language enables us as human beings to communicate with with one another and to participate in the life of one's community, but also because words beget actions and movement. There is no language that is not beautiful, not poetic, despite what detractors of particular languages say, with their sense of superiority, covering their ignorance, prejudice, or tin ear. However, there are people who resist learning the language of an historical enemy, of the conqueror and colonizer, because it was used like a whip across a population's back, an instrument of commands and orders, deculturation, and national humiliation.

Because English has been used as an important weapon in an occupying nation's arsenal of subjugation, I had to think long and hard about whether I should become an English teaching "aide" to students, most of whose home languages were already the result of colonial domination, the great majority in the ESL program at FCI Dublin being Spanish speakers. Most of these women are from Mexico or of Mexican heritage who have lived in the United States, some for nearly all their lives.

In my early teens I had picked up some Spanish here and there, but not enough to hold a conversation. Living in Texas, I should have studied it in high school, but in those days, French was the preferred language for those who hoped to go to an Eastern college or university. Later, in the 1970s while I was at the Federal Women's Prison at Alderson, I met Lolita Lebron, the Puerto Rican nationalist who, along with three other companeros had invaded the U.S,. Congress in 1954 in order to bring the demand for Puerto Rico's independence before the world. In the course of many conversations about the colonial status of Puerto Rico, the war in Vietnam, and the question of national liberation and decolonization, Lolita began to teach me some Spanish. But, because the process of learning Spanish was slow and we enjoyed talking together, we always ended up conversing in English. If I remember correctly, her generation of students had been forced to learn English in the schools in Puerto Rico. Spanish had been prohibited as the language of learning for a number of decades after the colonization by the United States.

Only after I was imprisoned again in 1985 did I finally learn Spanish well enough to communicate. In that period, during the government's battle against the cocaine cartels, there were times when nearly 75 percent of the women being held at Manhattan Correctional Center in New York were Spanish-speakers, most from Colombia. Few had enough English at their command to negotiate the difficult circumstances of being in a strange land in the worst possible situation. In prison a woman knows no one, has no person of confidence in her daily life to consult about what is going on around her and what might happen. Simple responses like "yes" or "no" can be compromising in complex situations, especially if one does not know what one is agreeing to, but is intimidated into giving some response!

I could not stand aside and be silent. For me, fairness is crucial to creating a world I wish to live in. As an anti-imperialist and anti-racist, I realized that I had to go beyond the ease of being in the predominantly English environment and enter the Spanish-speaking one. I had to overcome my own difficulties and embarrassment as a learner before I could support those isolated in a land familiar because of TV, but hostile. All foreign national women suffered culture shock and the shock of being in this distorted colony within America. All of us, U.S. residents included, were mourning our social death.

Besides getting a grammar book and a dictionary, I began to spend a lot of time with Latin American women. Nearly all were generous with their time and company, happy that someone wanted to learn Spanish in order to relate to their social context. Nevertheless I ran up against my own wall. Hanging like dark shadows over my actual learning process were feelings of inadequacy, even stupidity because I could not understand well or respond intelligibly – this is the kind of wall that other second language learners encounter within themselves. In the first months, even after I could comprehend some things, I had great trouble responding. What a blow, given my usual confidence in speaking! With a lot of encouragement, and frequent laughter at my unruly syntax and "gringo" pronunciation, I did slowly gain the ability and confidence to interpret, at least minimally, in critical situations: dialog with officers or other prisoners, letters from lawyers or the courts, rules and regulations.

As adults, most of us take for granted our competence, our ability to respond and interact effectively. My own problems in learning gave me insight into the vast leap that most of us must make to learn another language. Our brains must awaken to grasp vocabulary, syntax; our eyes must learn to recognize words and their roots; our ears must learn to hear multitudes of sound, not only of the words, but speech rhythms and the intonations and accents of the speaker; and our mouths must learn unfamiliar ways of moving our lips, tongues, jaws, along with new ways of using our breath to articulate what we wish to say and to put words in the proper order. Not so easy, and certainly a mountain to climb compared to the ease of learning our home language.

Reflecting on my own adult language-learning experience, I considered teaching in the prison's English program more seriously. I had the skills to teach, and philosophically I wanted to contribute to my sisters' general learning and experience in the present and their ability to negotiate and change their worlds in the future. To know the language of the dominant political, economic and military power may be decisive in living in what we now refer to as a globalized world. It is even more important for one simply trying to live and survive in the United States.

After having taught several intermediate and advanced classes, I was asked to step into a pre-beginner class, as the teacher of that class was preparing to leave on a writ for a court hearing. In this pre-beginner class, basic prison survival skills are taught as a part of life skills, with little emphasis on grammar. Grammar comes later, after the students have some vocabulary to begin to understand what is going on around them and to navigate the prison world, much as a traveler in a foreign country might have to do.

All the students spoke Spanish as their home language; the majority were from Mexico. The first week I spent getting to know the women. I wanted to learn about them, as students and as personalities and to put them at ease. I asked them to say something about themselves, their lives, where they were from. I also paid attention to their level of learning and to their attitudes toward learning in general and English in particular. I quickly figured out who the most and least advanced students were. I was pleased that most of them were eager to learn English—in fact, some had waited for several years to get into the class. But almost all were too embarrassed to try to speak in English on their own. A few had not advanced beyond third or fourth grade and were seriously hampered by their weak reading abilities and learning skills, though still anxious to face the challenge. One had become discouraged, having made little progress after more than a year as a "pre-beginner".

Then there were the two women who sat in the back of the classroom; Flor, who had been in the class a few months, and Delia, who had recently started. They and the other women in the class rarely engaged one another. Delia knew quite a bit of English and was in this class only until she could be tested and moved on. She would speak up briefly until Flor arrived, always late, and then fall silent, at least in English. But in Spanish she carried on, chatting animatedly with Flor in the back of the room. Flor told me later, in Spanish, that she and Delia had grown up together in a *caserio*—a housing project-in San Juan, Puerto Rico.

Because they were Puerto Ricans, and technically citizens of the United States, Flor and Delia were obliged by law to study English, in order not to lose "good time". Delia took an interest in improving her English literacy skills and was soon moved to a class at a higher level. Flor, showing few English skills, had to stay.

Flor continued sitting in the back row, now silent, doing her written class work without asking questions about the work, but readily allowing me to review what she'd done when I worked one-on-one with her. She would do her work quickly and quite well. It was clear that she understood more English than she would admit to, but she would never speak, except in Spanish.

In adult classes, a teacher must be able to encourage the most learning possible, without anyone embarrassing anyone, creating conflict, or hard feelings. And, as a prisoner teaching other prisoners, I was always careful about how I related to my students. We are equal as human beings, and even more equal as prisoners; I wanted to avoid any suggestion that as a "teacher," I was trying to be "over" another prisoner, or "pulling rank," either in school, or anywhere else. One of the most common responses in a situation where one prisoner says something that implies criticism of another about work, school, or anything is: *You're not the police; you're a number just like me so shut up.*

After several unsuccessful attempts to engage Flor in the class, I decided to take another tack. I realized that, because I had stepped into the middle of another teacher's class, I had not given my "talk" about learning English with which I usually began. Now I gave it:

Most of you speak Spanish and you may not have ever have required English to make life more bearable and intelligible in this prison world, since more than two-thirds of the population speak Spanish and even some in authority do. While some of you are anxious to learn English, others have no choice; you have to be in this class. I can understand why that might cause you to feel resentment or anger. Hopefully you'll decide you might as well learn this language. Why? To be able to participate in the world around you even though you are forced to be here. Yes, English is the language of the empire, the language of military occupation and economic denomination. If I were not an U.S. resident, I might not like English. I might not care about Shakespeare or other English writers, but I would want to know what these English speakers are up to.

Through language you understand what is being said to you or about you. And you can read what is being written about you, your family, your community, or your land. You have the power to detect the lies and to respond and defend yourself. Your home language nourishes and reinforces your people's right to self-determination, independence and justice as part of the culture and richness of the society. But knowing the language of the colonizer enables you to know more than he does. You have an edge; you know what the English speaker says and likely thinks, but he doesn't know what you say or think. Knowledge is a tool and language is a tool. In this world the more tools we have to build with, the better.

My students smiled; they understood what I said since I'd said it in English and in Spanish. Then class began. Flor remained quiet but she looked at me with her piercing green eyes, with curiosity, I thought. At the end of class, she did not run out the door as was her custom but waited until I had finished speaking with another student. Then Flor and I stepped outside onto the short path that led to the locked doors that open for the ten-minute movement from one area to another in the prison compound.

Miss, que sabe de colonialismo? [What do you know about colonialism?] I told her that I support Puerto Rican independence and have *independentista companeros*. She smiled.

The next days were no different. Flor continued to arrive late and maintain her silence. At last I approached her to say that since I believed she could speak some English, I was curious to know whether she refused to speak English for a reason. She smiled and nodded. She told me – in Spanish, of course – that she was the only one in her family who was an *independentista* in her heart. And she would not be forced to learn English or to speak it, even if she lost all her good time.

I argued that that was a terrible idea! What would her children say about that? She stayed on then, but eventually left ESL for a Spanish-language GED class. She didn't lose her good time; she found a loophole in the regulations. She knows that she will ultimately have to pass an exam proving that she can read and comprehend English. But for now, she does not have to study English.

Today in Puerto Rico, there is a great deal of distress about the state of the nation's language. In a manifesto, "United by Our Language," presented at the Center for Advanced studies in Puerto Rico and the Caribbean in April 2009, point 7 states: "That in spite of the resistance and strength that the Spanish language continues to have in Puerto Rico, there currently exists a profound, serious, preoccupation concerning the progressive deterioration of the vocabulary of Puerto Rican citizens, including basic linguistic skills in oral and written expression, as well as critical thinking" (Claridad, 2009).

The manifesto goes on to demand that the current policies be changed to "install a policy on Spanish-language learning that is compatible with the sociological and cultural reality of the Puerto Rican student body". Puerto Rico has resisted the imposition of a foreign language, English; but the mixing of it with Spanish, for many of the population, has impeded knowledge of either language adequately. The trampling on the language that unites this country with the rest of Latin America undermines the culture and identity of a proud nation. Citizens such as Flor recognize that, even without having graduated from high school.

We continue to talk nearly every day. I encourage Flor to work on her Spanish GED studies, then we talk about her country, her beloved green island, and her desire to participate in defending her proud nation.

REFERENCES

Claridad – Editorial Staff (2009) "Unido por nuestra idioma", *Claridad*, San Juan (Puerto Rico), translated by Marilyn Buck – May 7.

ABOUT THE AUTHOR

As a teenager in Texas *Marilyn Buck* joined movements to end the war in Vietnam and fight oppression of black people in the U.S. Later she actively supported anti-imperialist struggles and the Black Liberation Movement; in 1973 convicted of purchasing handgun ammunition, she was given a ten year sentence. After four years in Federal prison in Alderson, West Virginia, she was granted a furlough and went underground. Recaptured eight years later she was convicted of several politically motivated conspiracies and acts—including the freeing of Assata Shakur, now in political exile in Cuba. Marilyn's sentences totaled eighty years. In Dublin-FCI in California she became deeply involved in many projects, including HIV/AIDS education. Buck has won PEN awards for poetry and nonfiction. Among her collections of poetry is *Rescue the Word,* (2002); in 2008, City Lights Books published Buck's translation of Cristina Peri Rossi's *State of Exile,* which was her Master's thesis. She expects to be released in March, 2010.

Reflections on the Prison as Community
Judith Clark

The words, *prison,* and *community* are usually thought of as antithetical to each other. To be sentenced to serve time is to be removed from "the community" and sent "away" to prison. The nature of prison as an involuntary, isolated, guarded and oppressive institution runs counter to all that we associate with the notion of community. Yet, the very existence of this journal and many of its writings speaks to the ways that prisoners create community, often despite the prison's structure, rules and mores, and in so doing, reclaim and grow our humanity.

I have been incarcerated in Bedford Hills Correctional Facility, New York State's maximum-security prison for women, since 1983. For 20 years, from 1984-2004, Bedford was administered on an unusual basis that promoted the values of community. The prison was not viewed as an instrument of punishment—the punishment was coming to prison—but rather, as a community, albeit involuntary and guarded, in which everyone who lived *and* worked, was a member. While no prisoner chose to be here, each of us was challenged to decide who we wanted to become—what role we chose to play—in this community.

In many ways, Bedford was very much a traditional woman's prison, shaped by the history of reform and a recognition of the differences between female and male prisoners, that gave rise to women's reformatories in the early 20th century. Moreover, in the decade after Attica, many saw a shift toward promoting education and rehabilitative programs and developing administrative structures that were more responsive to prisoner's needs and rights. Throughout the 1970's, women at Bedford had successfully pursued class action suits which resulted in significant reforms including: ensuring their rights within the disciplinary process, a court ordered monitor of the medical and dental care, and specific privacy rights in relation to male officers. Perhaps most significantly, the Judge who ordered court monitoring of the disciplinary process also put the women who had brought the suit in charge of polling the entire facility to decide how the sizable fines levied against the facility should be met. Not only did this give unusual authority and respect to prisoners, but it also created a dynamic in which those women shifted from an adversarial relationship with the prison administration to a cooperative one on a practical level. All of this helped set the stage for the policies instituted by Superintendent Elaine Lord, who headed Bedford's administration from 1984 until 2004.

For a decade, the Bedford model was emblematic of a number of reform oriented prisons, particularly but not exclusively women's prisons. Then in the 1990's, the sky-rocketing numbers being sent to prison and the ratcheting up of the rhetoric in the "war on crime," resulted in a shift toward more punitive and bureaucratic models. Bedford bucked the trend for another decade, until a change in administration in 2004 gave way to a push for this prison to conform to other maximum-security men's prisons in the state system.

It is common to hear the "old prison" described as overly lenient, lax, and just too easy for a maximum security prison. Some say, askance, "the inmates ran the prison," or complain that it was too cushy to teach us our lesson and to keep us from coming back once released. But how then to explain the low recidivism rate for women who served long sentences at Bedford through this period? Why have so many of them gone into human services careers where they are serving their communities? Why were there so few incidents of serious violence and almost no intentional harm to staff? Without an atmosphere of overt threat and coercion, how did the prison function so well as to be recognized internationally as "a model prison"? I would argue that much of this success lies with the community model prison, and that superficial reactions to its seeming laxity miss the real workings of this model.

In this essay, I want to take a closer look at the community model prison that was Bedford Hills, to understand its operating principles, how it worked and some of the conflicts within the model. This is in no way "an objective study". I write as a participant and beneficiary of that model.

THE ETHOS OF COMMUNITY

The notion that everyone who lived or worked in the prison was part of one community turns on its head some basic relational assumptions of *Prison,* where the divide between *keepers* and *kept* is wide and adversarial. In reality, every prison is dependent upon inmate labor and most prisoners would rather work than sit idle and locked. But the dynamics of coercion obfuscate this reality. At Bedford, the value of everyone's work was recognized. Women were encouraged to take initiative and gained status through their work. There were women who facilitated groups, developed programs, maintained the facility as plumbers and carpenters, fixed electrical appliances as well as the wandering gardener. When the prison came under pressure to improve its mail room, trusted prisoners took on working there under civilian supervision. Over the years, these jobs grew into identities that everyone recognized and appreciated. Likewise, while there are often conflicts of interest between prison staff and prisoners, there are also overlapping interests in having the prison function well. In the community model, this latter reality was highlighted and encouraged, by maintaining informal lines of communication between staff and prisoners and encouraging far more interpersonal communication between staff and the women than is the norm in prisons, where relationships are formal and distant and informal interactions are suspect. This informal, interpersonal approach began at the top, with the Superintendent, who regularly walked the prison grounds, notepad in hand, and allowed anyone who wished to line up and talk to her. She also maintained an open door policy for security and civilian staff. Rules, searches, locks, control of movement and all the usual machinery of prison security were utilized regularly. But they were not the sole or primary way that order was maintained. Correctional Officers in charge of living units and work areas were respected for their communication skills and ability to problem-solve. They were encouraged to know "their women," to build rapport and make use of informal relationships to maintain calm and cleanliness and to talk a problem down, rather than rely on threat or force. Long-time officers also took pride in taking initiative and putting their individual stamp on their area of work. For example, officers who were in charge of processing visitors for many years, made a point of getting to know families and interact with the children, who were put at ease by this personal attention.

Civilian staff and volunteers were critical and valued members of the community. In addition to the teachers, counselors, and chaplains, all of the educational and therapeutic programs relied on strong oversight by civilian staff, many of whom played key roles in the lives of numerous women. A few, most notably Sister Elaine Roulet, the longtime director of the Children's Center, were guiding lights in fostering the sense of community and common concern for the whole facility. Bedford's many programs relied on hundreds of volunteers, who enabled program to function within budget limits. While relationships between staff and prisoners are usually suspect in prison, in the community model, the close bonds were seen as vital in providing informal mentoring, personal support and incentive to change. The volume and intensity of interaction between insiders and outsiders broke down the traditional isolation and insulation most prisoners experience and women actually grew in their sense of and participation in the larger society.

PRISONERS AS POTENTIAL RESOURCES

Recognizing incarcerated women as potential resources has enormous implications. That we were here because we were guilty of serious crimes was not forgotten, but we were not solely defined by our crimes. Our lives before prison were seen as more complex and that however we came into the prison, we had potential to grow and become productive. Thus, the depersonalization which is intrinsic to the dynamics of prison — assigning numbers, uniforms, congregate care, etc—was balanced by the environment in which each woman was encouraged to tell her unique story and to rewrite her story in different terms.

While the therapeutic model of recovery from addiction was a major element of the rehabilitative environment, there was also a strong developmental model, in which education, including college and vocational training, was promoted as a community value. This was highlighted every Spring, when Graduation Day was celebrated by the entire facility. Every woman who had achieved some advance in her vocational and academic courses participated. Graduates got to invite their families and friends. The gym was packed, from the rows of chairs for the graduates and honorees, to the bleachers from which women cheered, as the robed graduates marched in to celebratory mayhem. The event took hours, as each woman got her moment to walk on to the stage, often accompanied by her children. A woman who was struggling in her ABE class adult basic education – got to see her friends receive college degrees and say to herself, "one day that will be me". The youngster who kept getting in trouble and locked up watched her proud peers complete their state apprenticeships and felt a desire to find a new direction. The community's role was highlighted, as teachers, aides, civilian and prisoner volunteer tutors were thanked, along with families.

BUILDING COMMUNITY AND
BECOMING PART OF THE SOLUTION

The women's investment in taking responsibility for their own change was enhanced by illuminating the social context of people's personal problems, be they the drug culture, health or issues of violence. Under the rubric of "inmate centered programming," women were encouraged to address their personal problems through coming together to create community and programs, which could serve our needs and affect social change.

The policy of inmate centered programming began with The Children's Center, a multi-faceted program and community which involved the majority of the population, who are mothers. Many, many women, along with civilian staff and volunteers worked to ensure visits in a comfortable, child centered playroom, developed parenting classes and support groups, advocacy and phone calls, making of cards, tapes and every other means possible to enhance the mother-child bonds. We were challenged to recognize how we had harmed our children by our actions and to take responsibility as mothers to be a resource to them in coping with their lives and our incarceration. Women who initially utilized the resources of the Children's Center often became active in developing and facilitating its programs.

Our response to the early AIDS epidemic offers another instance of this community mobilization approach. As in all prisons, fear and ignorance fueled conflict, stigma and rumors, as those suspected of being infected were shunned and sometimes attacked. At the same time, unsafe behaviors, such as sharing needles and unsafe sex posed enormous risk. While other prisons maintained policies of containment, at Bedford, a group of women who were given permission to meet, broke the stranglehold of silence by voicing how AIDS was affecting them personally. We underwent an intensive process of education and mutual support, while reaching out to women in the infirmary and others. In cooperation with the administration and staff, we developed an outreach program of education, skits, songs and speaking out, which raised consciousness and built a spirit of sisterhood and support, throughout the facility. ACE—AIDS Education and Counselling— the organization which grew out of this mobilization, became a model for programs throughout the country. Women who had always felt themselves to be "a problem" experienced being "part of the solution," and this proved life-changing.

Community mobilization again promoted individual and social change when a group of women, with staff support, organized public hearings within the prison where they testified to their experiences of childhood and spousal abuse to audiences that included judges, legislators, district attorneys and others. These hearings helped raise public awareness of the impact of violence against women and children on crime, addiction and other social ills, and they promoted changes in laws and public policies. They created the Family Violence Program, which continues to provide individual and group counseling and support.

Community mobilization was utilized even to address security problems. For example, there were a few incidents of serious interpersonal violence and sexual abuse. While those involved faced the normal disciplinary repercussions, the administration also assembled a group of women active in programs addressing these issues and went around to every living unit, holding mandatory meetings to discuss how people felt about what had happened and how to address problems of intimidation, violence and abuse. Always it came down to the question, "how do we want to live with each other?" What avenues of redress can we use? What values and behaviors do we want to promote? Certainly, this did not consolidate a unified commitment to non-violence and respect, but it challenged everyone to see themselves as active participants in shaping community standards.

LIMITS

The hierarchy and ethos of security was never absent from Bedford, nor was it fully integrated into the community model operations. Rather, there was an uneasy fluctuation between the two outlooks, in terms of how policy was instituted. For example, while women were given unusual latitude to create and lead innovative programs, at some point, the administration would intervene to modify that grass roots effort, by bringing in civilian staff who were accountable to the prison hierarchy. Some of these transitions were smooth, while others involved varied levels of repression. We had to learn the limits of our "empowerment", and learned that strong civilian supervision was critical to the long-term stability of programs.

While cooperation between staff and prisoners proved enormously productive, the relationship and accountability was never mutual. The needs and power relations of the prison predominated, and every prisoner experienced the "pains of imprisonment" on a daily basis. The informal style of management could at any time lead to sudden, inexplicable changes that left us feeling blind-sided, angry and disoriented. We had to learn to ride those waves by developing a strong sense of what was important over the long run.

WHY IT WORKED

The community model worked because it represented an investment in and development of human potential. It relied on the strength of relationship-building, and the ethos of inter-dependence, rather than solely, force and control. The result was that women who came to prison with long histories of social marginalization and feelings of alienation, became stake-holders and active participants in our community. Women underwent profound changes in identity that lasted into their lives on the outside. The communal sense of responsibility produced a positive environment in the prison and in the larger society.

ABOUT THE AUTHOR

Growing up in Brooklyn, New York, *Judith Clark* was deeply involved in social protest movements in her teens. "Unwilling to heed the moderating influences of aging, changing conditions, or even motherhood", she says, she was arrested in 1981 for participating in an attempted robbery of a Brinks truck, in which three people were killed. She is serving a sentence of seventy-five years to life in Bedford Hills Correctional Facility. She earned her BA and MA at BHCF and helped to rebuild a college program when public funds were rescinded. She recently received her certification as a chaplain and currently works with the nursery mothers and raises service dogs for returning veterans in the *Puppies Behind Bars* program.

Much of Judith's work comes from her attempt to reckon with and take responsibility for her crime. Her poetry has appeared in *The New Yorker*, *Aliens at the Border*, *Doing Time*, and *Bridges*. Her scholarly work includes pieces in *The Prison Journal* and *Zero to Three*. She is co-author of *Breaking the Walls of Silence: Women and AIDS in a Maximum Security Prison*. For a complete listing of her writings, go to: www.judithclark.org.

PCAP:
A Voice from the Landfill
Kinnari Jivani

landfill /la'ndfil/ n. 1 a place where society's rejects are dumped to decompose, out of sight and silenced, etc. 2 a place where one could easily get buried and lost.

I live in a landfill known as prison.

In the United States most prisons are known as correctional facilities – the word corrections implying punishment and rehabilitation. But in most states, because of budget cuts, most of the educational and beneficial rehabilitation programs are cut off, and prisons have become human landfills or human warehouses.

The Pew Center on the States (2008) says that 1 in every 100 people in America are in prison (approximately 2.8 to 3 million people). With so many people living in concrete closets behind razor wire fences a big chunk of our individual and collective voice is silenced. Behind the metal doors loads of raw potential lie buried.

Prison Creative Arts Project (PCAP), a non profit organization founded in 1990, recognizes the raw potential, and provides positive outlets for men and women incarcerated in Michigan through a multitude of art forms. PCAP also works with juvenile facilities and has a Linkage program for prisoners returning to the community. PCAP's administrators and volunteers through their dedication and selfless service, create a space for us to share our voice, vulnerability, visions and talents with the outside world.

When I first came to prison each day was like a thousand years long and I didn't know if I would make it to the next day. The pain that my actions caused to the other people haunted me and I didn't know how to continue to live on. Nine years later, I can testify how art has helped me cope with guilt, sorrow, frustration, shame and loss. How I sketched and wrote page after page trying to make sense of it all! How a mere pen, pencil, and paper kept me sane! My art became my meditation, my prayer, my savior. I would never have considered myself an artist or a writer, but PCAP changed that.

The first year I was in prison, a fellow prisoner urged me to submit my sketches to the art exhibition held by PCAP. My sketches were primitive and I was sure they would be rejected, but to my surprise the curators selected one of the sketches, vitalizing me to continue drawing. The next year I experimented with color pencils and pastels, and the following year I tried paints. My artwork continued to improve. I also gathered up enough courage to sign up for a poetry writing workshop. English is not my first or second language and I was unsure of myself, my words and my ability to write something authentic that others would find worth reading. Once I joined the workshop I was relieved – the volunteers and the group members created the space that felt safe and nurturing. Every week we entered the workshop like it was a temple, carrying our unique offerings, unique experiences and styles. We wrote and shared our pain, fear, hopes and dreams. We inspired and challenged each other to rise to a new level. We called our group SOUL (Sisters of Unique Lyrics). In our writing sisterhood, I didn't just become a better writer but also a better person, and I will always be grateful.

A few months ago, I was moved to Huron Valley Correctional Facility, where I joined PCAP's art and theater workshops. The first is an energized space where we meet to create our own works. In "Sisters Within", the theater workshop, we sit in a circle sharing our intimate stories. We have taken risks and exposed our raw emotions. Now we are creating scenes based on our stories and making a play that in coming months we can perform in front of an audience. In the process we are reflecting, developing insights and growing.

As I write and paint, I continue to heal and explore myself. I wonder where I would be if I never had an opportunity to share my art, my voice – would I have become bitter for being forever despised by society? Would I have suffocated in these concrete closets and withered away into nothingness? Thank goodness for organizations like PCAP! Because of them my time in Prison has not been spent decomposing, instead I have blossomed. Through PCAP, my writings have been published. My art work has traveled to the National STOPMAX conference in Philadelphia and received an Environmental Service Award for artistic contribution to the United Nations' Wise World Environmental Day in California. Each year for two weeks my artwork hangs in the gallery at the Annual Art Exhibition at the University of Michigan, Ann Arbor, alongside the remarkable works of hundreds of men and women incarcerated across the state.

People from all roads of life come and view our works. They read our statements or pick up the anthologies of our writings, they hear our voices, see our painted emotions and thoughts, and perhaps for a moment they see us more than a litany of our worst acts; they see us as artists and writers, and more than anything as human beings. And in those moments a bridge is built.

bridge /brij/ n. & v. • n. 1 a structure that connects one to another. b a layout that links lost voices from landfills back to mainstream.

PCAP is a bridge that helps prisoners rediscover and reconnect to themselves and to the community. I am blessed to have access to such a valued bridge.

REFERENCES

Pew Center on the States (2008) *One in 100: Behind Bars in America 2008,* Washington: The Pew Charitable Trusts – February. Retrieved from http://www. pewcenteronthestates.org/uploadedFiles/8015PCTS_Prison08_FINAL_2-1-1_ FORWEB.pdf.

ABOUT THE AUTHOR

Kinnari Jivani was born and raised in India. She is fluent in Gujarati, Hindi and English. She has a B.S. In microbiology from the University of Mumbai. At the age of 20, she was arrested, then sentenced to 11 to 20 years of imprisonment in Michigan. Her earliest release date is in January 2001, after which she faces deportation. Since her incarceration she has been discovering and exploring her talent for painting and writing. Her artwork has been featured in the Michigan Bar Journal and the Artist Magazine. Her paintings have been shown in the Annual Exhibition of Art by Michigan Prisoners for many years and has consistently won first place awards. Her writings have been published in *The Change Agent,* a magazine for social change; *A Crack in the Concrete,* an anthology of poems; *Bhumika,* a feminist magazine; *The Project V-Day: Until the Violence Stops,* headed by Eve Ensler; and in the *Michigan Review of Prisoner Creative Writing*, an anthology. She is a yoga instructor and volunteers weekly yogasana classes in the facility. She is now housed in the Women's Huron Valley Correctional Facility in Michigan.

The Evolution of the Prison Creative Arts Project
Buzz Alexander

The Prison Creative Arts Project (PCAP) originated by accident in January 1990. A student enrolled in my course on guerrilla theater asked if two lifers at the women's prison an hour and a half away could take the course. They were University of Michigan students, and she was carrying course materials to them. I said yes, and she, I, and a second student traveled to the prison once a week, talking theater and prison, and doing improv acting. An exercise gave the two women opportunity to ask us direct questions about our presence and challenge us with situations they faced in prison. We answered honestly if imperfectly. At the end, they looked at each other and said "we have to open this to the entire prison". The warden approved, and the group that formed, the Sisters Within Theater Troupe, is, twenty years later, working on their twenty-eighth play. I am still a proud member.

PCAP grew slowly from there. The Sisters' first play, a collection of monologs, dialogues, and scenes, was performed at the prison on April 28, 1991. The course added three new prisons in the winter of 1992, invited by a lifers' group in a men's prison and by an assistant deputy warden at another prison; we initiated the contact at the third prison. From the start somehow we knew not to send requests up through prison officials to the Michigan Department of Corrections (MDOC) in Lansing. We stayed local, doing quality programs at the prisons. In 1990, I and some student volunteers had begun a video project with children at the Dewey Center for Urban Education in Detroit, a school serving local housing projects. In 1993, we moved from there to a Detroit high school. In 1994, we had our first plays in the high school and in two juvenile facilities. In 1995, Janie Paul and I invited artists from prisons within a 200 mile radius of Ann Arbor to submit work for an exhibition. We were stunned by the volume of response and the quality of the art already being created. In February 1996, 50 artists exhibited 77 works of art; 462 visitors saw the exhibition in eight days. Janie's School of Art and Design course, "Art Workshops in Prisons", in 1995 began to send art students to juvenile facilities and prisons. By 1998, we had started up poetry workshops in the prisons and juvenile facilities. We also facilitated dance, music, photography, and video projects, mostly in the high schools. We changed our name from the Prison Theater Project to the Prison Creative Arts Project in 1995 and by 1997 had formalized our meetings, though we were still an organization of only about 20 members.

In 1999, I was finally summoned to Lansing by the Deputy Director of the MDOC. Our workshops had been noticed. He approved of the exhibition, he told me, but was suspicious of our theater work. We worked out that I would create and send him a mission statement, and that we would submit our scenarios for approval. Before I could comply, however, he shut down our theater workshops and would not respond to my messages. After waiting nearly a month, we contacted the Director of Political Relations for the University and a state senator. When they asked him for a meeting he opened the workshops again, though denied permission to continue our dance workshop at the women's prison. Because of this experience, we established a National Advisory Board, our own separate mission statement, an elected executive committee, and a speakers bureau. We had realized that we needed to be ready to articulate and defend ourselves. We also began to strengthen our ties with sympathetic wardens – one of whom agreed to serve on our Advisory Board – and other leaders within the MDOC.

In 2010, we will celebrate twenty years as an organization with a Symposium during the Fifteenth Annual Exhibition of Art by Michigan Prisoners. Some of our 166 PCAP Associates, graduates who are doing social justice work across the country, will participate. Our accomplishments at this point are as follows: the youth and adults in our workshops have now created 506 original plays; they have given 182 readings, including 116 in the prisons; they have participated in over 125 art workshops; in the Fourteenth Annual Exhibition of Art by Michigan Prisoners 229 artists exhibited 390 works of art, and 4,069 visitors walked through the gallery in two weeks – a wall and a half of the gallery held works on climate change and another small wall had a variety of portraits of Barak Obama, and we continued a long-standing practice of panels and guest speakers; we have held eleven exhibitions of art by incarcerated youth; since 2001, in our Portfolio Project we work one on one with incarcerated youth as they create handsome portfolios of their art and writing; since 2001, our Linkage Project has connected returning youth and adults with community arts mentors; our speakers bureau has addressed a wide range of audiences, both local and national; in 2009, we produced our first number of *On Words: Michigan Review of Prisoner Creative Writing*; the National Endowment for the Arts gave us an Access Grant, because we give access to the arts to those who don't normally have it; the Rockefeller Foundation awarded us a PACT Grant because our work is community-based; the Office of the Provost, the

College of Literature, Science & the Arts, the School of Art and Design, and the Department of English Language have funded us for a 3 year period beginning in 2008; and we have excellent relations with the top leadership in the Michigan Department of Corrections.

What has sustained us?

Perhaps most important is the way we work. We admire the artists, writers, dancers, musicians, and actors we work with. We are in awe of their talents, their resistance to their conditions, and their efforts to grow into the people they want to be. We try to be as creative and authentic as they. We are not their teachers but people who enter equally into a creative space that wouldn't exist if we weren't there, then write, perform, and risk creativity with everyone in the space. We trust the processes of the workshops in the facilities and schools. We feel no need to dominate or control. We believe in the participants in the workshops and exhibitions, no matter how problematic a group, a workshop, or an individual may become at any given moment.

The same trust and belief, the same pedagogy, if you will, occurs in our courses: Art and Design 310, English 310 – workshops in any of the arts in high schools and juvenile facilities, English 319 – theater workshops in high schools, juvenile facilities, and prisons, and English 326 – the portfolio course. All course workshops and ninety percent of PCAP workshops are student-run. After two weeks of orientation – exercises in the arts, briefings on rules and regulations, answering questions – students enter the creative space. They share their experience with each other, and we listen and offer advice through weekly journal responses, team meetings, and intense classroom discussions. After a course, students can join PCAP. Every two weeks PCAP meets and small consistent groups offer feedback.

We are highly responsible and know what is at stake. We adhere to the rules and regulations of the facilities. We understand genuine security concerns and agree that everyone in a prison or youth facility needs to be safe. We respectfully negotiate the differences between security language and our creative language, and the aura we bring with us. We respect both those who are housed in these institutions and those who work there. We continue to be welcomed because of our professionalism, because we own up to our mistakes and rectify them, and because we do quality work. We continue to earn support from the university, again because of quality, responsible work, and because of the deep effect on the lives and careers of our students.

We recognize how mass incarceration has devastated lives and neighborhoods in this country, and we understand the causes of this mass incarceration. Some of us are fueled by anger at what has been done in our name, others by a personal existential need to work at the side of the oppressed, others by the courage and resistance they learn from prison actors, artists, and writers, others by a hope for organized change, others by religious faith. We bring to the work a deep and thoughtful commitment.

We were featured as a model program at the Philadelphia Mural Arts' Arts in Criminal Justice Conference in October 2007; we have participated in an effort to create a national coalition of prison arts programs; we are eager to provide (unpaid) internships and to share our experience as well as knowledge with anyone starting out and any developed program; we are eager to learn how to better our own practice.

ABOUT THE AUTHOR

Buzz Alexander is an Arthur F. Thurnau Professor of English Language and Literature at the University of Michigan as well as founder and member of the ground-breaking Prison Creative Arts Project. He has received the Amoco Good Teaching Award, the University of Michigan Regents' Award for Distinguished Public Service, and the Harold R. Johnson Diversity Service Award. In 2005, he received the Carnegie Foundation for the Advancement of Teaching and Council for the Advancement and Support of Education Professor of the Year Award. His books include *Film on the Left; American Documentary Film from 1931-1942* (Princeton University Press, 1981) which was nominated for a Pulitzer Prize in History and was winner of the Theatre Library Association Award for best film book of 1981. His book about PCAP, *Is William Martinez Not Our Brother?,* will be published by the University of Michigan Press in 2010.

BREAKING INTO PRISON WITH CAMERAS: DOCUMENTARY FILMMAKERS TESTIFY

Writ-Writer:
One Man's Journey for Justice
Susanne Mason

There is no shortage of prison stories to be told: the themes of redemption and revenge, of unexpected kindness and justice denied make life behind prison walls a treasure trove of drama. But too many of the stories will never be told – the walls work both ways. Filmmakers trying to get access to prison have abandoned many proposed projects because of the formidable roadblocks and byzantine bureaucratic hurdles erected by prison officials. One result is that the public has little idea how existing prison practices and policies affect the millions of incarcerated Americans, and how their plight is central to larger, more critical criminal justice issues.

No other segment of American society erects such formidable barriers to inspection. It is left to the dedicated journalist or documentary filmmakers to bang at prison walls and tell the necessary stories. But they will be stalled and frustrated, and may spend weeks, months, and sometimes years trying to produce the reports and documentation needed to communicate to the free world what is going on in prison or what has already happened behind the walls.

My experience making two documentaries that required filming inside the Texas prison system taught me one thing very quickly: time is on the prison administration's side, unless you are a network anchor or famous television news reporter.

If you're not famous; if you're an unknown documentary filmmaker, the emotional toll of gaining access becomes a huge part of the work itself. I once worked for more than six months to get permission for a five-day prison shoot. On the third day of the shoot I was notified that we would have to wrap up by lunchtime the next day. A TV network anchor and his crew needed to cover an upcoming execution. If I had insisted, I *may* have been granted permission for a second shoot, but I didn't have the funds to produce it.

In 1990, I began preparations for a documentary about domestic violence. The issue would be shown through the stories of several women incarcerated for murdering men who, by their accounts, had abused and threatened to kill them. The only logistical challenge was obtaining permission to videotape and interview the women prisoners in the Riverside Unit in Gatesville. The warden, a woman, was sympathetic to the issue at the heart of the women's stories – the possibility that they had killed in self-defense. After writing a request letter and talking to her on the phone, she granted me access, provided that I get additional approval from Huntsville.

I knew enough about the Texas prison system to know that this would be a big hurdle. The warden didn't know whom the proper clearance should come from, only that I must have it. I made a lot of phone calls and left a lot of messages that weren't returned and made more phone calls, and eventually got somebody to call back. I pushed for and was granted a meeting in Huntsville.

The official said I could videotape the women for my documentary, but that prior to distribution, I needed their approving sign-off. I wasn't willing to drop the film project over this. I had spent months researching the issue and corresponding with the women whom I planned to interview. When prison officials sent me the written agreement, I crossed out the language about final approval, initialed and signed it, and mailed it back. I notified the warden that I had official permission, recruited my crew, and we set shooting dates.

Warden Cranford then denied me permission to videotape the women in their prison dormitories or at their job posts. I would only be allowed to interview them in an empty classroom in a separate building. I thought, how can I make a documentary film if all the audience sees is talking heads? Wouldn't I simply be editing a series of interviews together? Was this limitation designed to dissuade me from making the film?

I wrote her a long letter explaining how critical it was that the film show the women in their everyday prison lives. She wouldn't budge, except to allow me to take still photographs of each of the women in posed positions following the interviews. In the end, I used those stills, video exteriors of the prison, and family photos of the women and made the movie the best I could. Titled *Stories from the Riverside*, the film was one of the first to look at the self-defense angle of domestic homicide by women. Fortunately, it was picked up by a reputable educational distributor and used widely by organizations working to educate the public about family violence.

My next film was a prison story I knew would never be told on film, except by a filmmaker like me – green, passionate about the subject, and eager to sink my teeth into a serious production. Had I known the level of difficulty the film presented I don't think I would have taken it on. Thankfully, eagerness trumped good sense, because the film was ultimately broadcast nationally on PBS and honored by national organizations.

Before it was finished it had at least three working titles – but *Writ Writer* stuck. It is a historical documentary about the civil rights era prison reform litigation in Texas prisons and tells the history primarily from the prisoners' perspective. It offers a powerful view of the transformation of one state prison system during the 1960s, as prisoners nationwide began to enjoy greater access to federal courts as a result of several Supreme Court rulings.

The central figure in the history is a prisoner named Fred Arispe Cruz, who waged a legal battle on several fronts against the Texas Department of Corrections in the 1960s. In a larger sense, Cruz fought to sever the roots of plantation slavery that had shaped the Texas prison system since its founding. His determination earned him long bouts of solitary confinement and other retaliatory punishments.

To portray the atmosphere of Texas prisons in the fifties and sixties I would use both archival film footage and modern-day film footage shot by me and my crew. To do that, I needed permission from the prison system to film inside the walls and fences. This time, I went straight to the top and met with the executive director of the Texas Department of Criminal Justice (TDCJ) to request permission to film. He granted it and instructed me to work out the particulars with the Institutional Division director and the Public Information office. By the time I had my first meeting with my assigned PI officer, I had spent months waiting for access, and it would still take another three months to get shooting dates set.

This time, I was able to interview two prisoners who knew Cruz while incarcerated in the sixties and film general prison activity inside the Ellis Unit, in the cotton fields, inside the gin and in the gym. The footage would cut interchangeably with archival film of the fifties, sixties and seventies. It would enhance the visual and artistic quality of the film, making it more attractive to national distributors. In turn, millions of people might eventually see *Writ Writer* and learn of Cruz's efforts.

The most frustrating experience in making *Writ Writer* was obtaining mug shots of prisoners featured in the film. These are public records, and the TDCJ had released paper copies of them to me. When I asked for the actual photos, and agreed to pay for the cost of providing them, two officials, one who said no and the other who said yes, spent a year bouncing me back and forth. It was an enormous waste of my time and money, and an example of how prison administrators dissuade film producers because they can. In desperation I contacted an advisor who happened to know the chief counsel at TDCJ and offered to call him. He graciously heard my grievance and instructed the records officials to let me have the photos. Game over.

Needless to say, these two officials were not happy with me and dragged their heels when I called to make arrangements to photograph the microfilmed mugs, on site in Huntsville, three hours drive-time away. When I arrived, neither of the two records officials were available. A state employee showed me the cubicle where the microfilms were waiting. I checked to see if everything had been pulled and discovered that several mug shots were missing. I think this was their revenge. One of the missing mugs was of a famous and notoriously violent building tender – a prisoner recruited by the warden to act as a guard over other prisoners. This prisoner "knew where the bodies were buried". Even 25 years after his death, the "good old boys" of the prison system still guarded his image, part of the sordid history of the TDCJ. No matter how long it might take and what obstacles I had to overcome, the story I was telling was part of that history and needed to be told.

ABOUT THE AUTHOR

Susanne Mason's new documentary Writ Writer was broadcast nationally on the Emmy Award-winning PBS series Independent Lens in Summer 2008 and received the prestigious 2009 Silver Gavel Award from the American Bar Association. She has served as associate producer of a variety of PBS documentaries, including *Are the Kids Alright?*, *Struggle in the Fields*, *Songs of the Homeland*, and *Go Back to Mexico!* Mason received a Silver Apple from the National Educational Film & Video Festival and a Director's Choice Award from the Black Maria Film & Video Festival, among other honors, for her film, *Stories from the Riverside* (1993), a 28-minute documentary about domestic homicide from the perspective of three women incarcerated for murdering their abusive husbands.

For more information, please visit:
www.writwritermovie.com
www.newday.com/films/writwriter.html

Deadline
Katy Chevigny

L ike many documentaries, Big Mouth's documentary "Deadline" shifted course many times during its making. The director and cinematographer Kirsten Johnson and I had decided to collaborate on a film project about capital punishment, and we wanted to offer a fresh perspective on a thorny topic that had been the subject of many other films. We knew how difficult it was to get permission to film in courtrooms and in prisons, but we didn't want to make a film that consisted entirely of so-called "talking heads", such as lawyers explaining casework. So we puzzled over a new approach.

Our first idea was to tell the story of a significant episode in the history of capital punishment, the 1972 *Furman v. Georgia* Supreme Court decision, which had temporarily abolished the death penalty nationwide. We planned to do some research to follow what happened to the more than 600 people who had their sentences commuted to life without parole. After some initial research, in the fall of 2002 we traveled to Mississippi, Alabama and Georgia to interview former death row prisoners and others involved in the Furman decision. One of our advisers for the film, George Kendall, recommended that we include some contemporary story element to contrast with the Furman story. "There's a lot of interesting things going on in Illinois right now", he reminded us.

We were aware of the developing story in Illinois, but hadn't intended to include it in our film. The background was this: Governor George Ryan had walked into office in 1999 only to discover that a lot of innocent people on Death Row had been wrongly convicted. And it was his job to authorize executions for those sentenced to death. Early in Ryan's term as governor, Anthony Porter was found to be innocent just two days before he was supposed to have been executed. Illinois had executed 12 people since the reinstitution of the death penalty in 1977 but had been forced to release 13 people because of new evidence. Ryan was dismayed by these facts, and in 2000 he had put a moratorium on executions, while also appointing a state commission to review the system and make recommendations. How did all this fit into our film about Furman? We had no idea, and as far as we were concerned, it didn't.

Coming back from Atlanta in 2002, I got a phone call from a friend who worked in public radio in Chicago, who said, "Aren't you making a film about the death penalty? Why aren't you here filming these hearings the Governor set up?" In his last months in office, Ryan asked the Illinois parole board to hold special extrajudicial hearings to review each of the 167 clemency claims of the people on Illinois' Death Row. It was news to us that the hearings were open to cameras, but we were well aware of the rarity of getting permission to film anything related to a capital punishment trial, so it piqued our interest. At the last minute, while the hearings were underway, Kirsten and I flew to Chicago for three days to film them and see if we could make anything of it. It was the documentarian's hunger for unusual access that was what ultimately motivated us. Filming something like a death penalty trial? Too good an opportunity to pass up.

It turned out that the way that the clemency hearings were set up was inherently dramatic, not to mention unprecedented and therefore historic. Ryan asked that the parole board hold an individual hearing for each of the 167 people currently on Death Row in Illinois. The parole board gave each case one hour, which was divided into 30 minutes for the prosecution and 30 minutes for the defense. From a film-making standpoint, it was pretty much a dream scenario: all the most salient and dramatic details of each case were distilled down to sixty minutes of contrasting argument and storytelling. We filmed for 3 days, 18 hearings, and had more than enough material for several complicated documentaries. The hearing room was often packed: with media, with family members of the victims as well as the prisoners' families, on occasion. Appellate lawyers and D.A.'s were sometimes handling several hearings a day. One day we heard the astonishing testimony of the case of Robert Jones. Jones was convicted of committing a gruesome double murder in a tight-knit community in rural Illinois. The audience listened rapt to several tearful testimonies of grieving family members of the victims. The next half hour featured the unexpected counter-testimony of the victim's neighbor, Jones' mother, who asked forgiveness of the family she had known her whole life. To everyone's amazement, the father of the victim replied directly to Jones' mother, breaking down as he described his futile attempts to try to forgive Jones' actions. And this was just one of 166 stories.

The only people who were conspicuously absent from the hearings were the Death Row prisoners themselves, who were not granted access to their own clemency hearings. As documentary filmmakers, we felt that a major piece of the story was missing. The protagonists themselves, the very people whose fate the Governor was agonizing over, were invisible to our cameras. We needed to get permission to film inside the prison, to see these central characters and hear their voices.

Getting permission to film inside prison is never easy. The rules for filming in a prison vary with each institution. In addition to whatever the stated rules are, the warden or corrections official responsible for publicity tends to have broad powers to grant or deny access at their discretion. In our experience, if the persons in charge didn't like the sound of your film project, they could deny you indefinitely.

In Illinois, however, there was already a lot of media attention on the prisons, and particularly on the prisoners on Death Row. In 2000 and 2001, several highly publicized exonerations of men on Death Row in Illinois had received national television news coverage. And to produce a special show on Illinois death row inmates, Oprah had recently gained access to film a portion of her daytime television show on Death Row. Since the media had been largely critical of flaws in the system, prison officials were on the defensive whenever they received a request to film.

Our Associate Producer, Angela Tucker, took on the responsibility of seeking permission from Illinois prison officials. Most of the time the answer she got was a flat out "no" to whatever she requested. First, we were told that there was a rule that no cameras were allowed on Death Row at all – the Oprah special being the notable exception – which essentially meant that there could be no new media coverage of the 167 people whose fates were in the hands of the deliberating Governor. We tried different tacks, explaining that we were showing all sides of the story, but we were told there was no way around the new "rule" of no cameras on Death Row.

At the same time that Angela was seeking permission to film, we were also scraping up funds to fly back and forth to Chicago in order to follow the Governor's mercurial decision-making process. One day the Governor told a press conference that he had taken the idea of a "blanket" commutation off the table. A couple of weeks later we filmed a historic relay march of exonerated men from all parts of the country through the night from Illinois' "Death House" to the State of Illinois building, where they presented the governor with a petition to commute the sentences of all 167 prisoners from death to life sentences. We had no idea how the story would end, but now we were hooked on it, and determined to follow through until the Governor did make a decision.

The Governor, though, had a deadline, which was his last day in office on January 13, 2003. He had to exercise his executive power before then. This was a relief to us filming, since we had been swept along with the drama of the Governor's deliberations, but didn't have the budget to follow it indefinitely. The advocates for commutation, led by the Center for Wrongful Convictions, was also running out of cash in their campaign to win hearts and minds – and specifically the Governor's – with a vision of mercy toward those on Death Row.

On January 11, 2003 we made another trip to Chicago to film Governor Ryan making history when he surprised the world by commuting the sentences of all 167 people on Death Row. We knew then that we had a new opportunity to film with the prisoners whose clemency hearings we had filmed, since the Death Row rule no longer applied.

Angela stayed in touch with her public affairs contact at the Illinois Department of Corrections and found out where the prisoners were transferred once they were moved off Death Row into the general population. Many were sent to other facilities around Illinois. Once we had obtained written permission from the prisoners themselves, the Department of Corrections granted us access to film. Gratefully, we traveled to Illinois one more time, to film interviews about the experiences of the prisoners themselves. Some, like Grayland Johnson and Gabriel Solache, claimed their innocence; others, like Robert Jones freely admitted their guilt. Having these disparate voices enabled us to make a film that documented a fascinating new chapter in the history of capital punishment, one worthy of being compared to the famous *Furman v. Georgia* case from 30 years earlier. And when the interviews were complete, we came back to New York to combine the stories of the two events into the film that became *Deadline*.

ABOUT THE AUTHOR

Katy Chevigny is co-director of *Deadline* (2004), an Emmy-nominated documentary, which premiered at the Sundance Film Festival and won the Thurgood Marshall Journalism Award. In an unusual acquisition of an independent film by a major television network, NBC broadcast DEADLINE as a primetime special on their Dateline series in 2004. She directed *Election Day* (2007), which screened at Toronto's Hot Docs Film Festival in 2007, and was broadcast on U.S. public television in 2008. Chevigny is also the co-founder and Executive Director of Arts Engine, Inc., a non-profit that supports, produces, and distributes independent media of consequence. These films and others produced by Big Mouth Films can be found at www.artsengine.net/store. Arts Engine's projects include Media Rights (see www.mediarights.org) and the Media That Matters Film Festival.

Angola Prison Hospice:
Opening the Door
Edgar Barens

My initial foray into documenting the criminal justice system began soon after my brother and his wife moved to a small town in Minnesota. I was a graduate student and eager to make socially relevant documentaries. Having been raised in a politically active family I ventured into film to direct documentaries that, with any luck, would cause positive change in the world.

The town my brother's family moved to was known for its state-of-the-art agricultural campus. They enjoyed the small town hustle and bustle bolstered by the diversity of the student body and bought a nice home to raise their family. Unbeknownst to the townsfolk, however, plans were being made by the University of Minnesota to sell the campus off to the Minnesota Department of Corrections (MDOC) to create a medium security prison.

Seeing the urgency to document the process of a rural community being transformed suddenly into a prison town, a small group of prison-opposing folks asked me to film the emotional community meetings and to document the underhanded practices of some of the town fathers and correctional officials. Once it became evident that the conversion from institution of higher learning to medium security prison was a "done deal", I was also at hand to document the final graduation ceremony at the closing campus.

The documentary that emerged, *Final Graduation*, attested to efforts to combat the sale of this cherished educational institution to the Department of Corrections and became an organizing tool for the prison-opposing folks in town. Sadly, despite their efforts, the people lost their battle against the MDOC, and the once bustling agricultural campus became a medium security prison within a stone's throw from a residential neighborhood. A few years later in New York City this experience of film-making would open doors allowing me to continue my work with the criminal justice system.

Of the many temporary jobs I had while living in New York City the best one was with the Open Society Institute (OSI), an organization founded by philanthropist George Soros. OSI implements a range of initiatives to advance justice, education, public health and independent media, and I was fortunate to have landed an entry-level position with OSI's Center on Crime, Communities, and Culture.

Partly because of my work on *Final Graduation*, OSI gave me the opportunity to direct a short documentary for the First National Conference on Death and Dying in Prisons and Jails. The Center on Crime, Communities, and Culture, and OSI's Project on Death in America co-sponsored the conference to begin a dialog on how jails and prisons address end-of-life issues.

My task was to create a nuts and bolts documentary on establishing a prison hospice. At that time (1999), only a handful of prison-based hospices were up and running. The Louisiana State Penitentiary in Angola (LSP-Angola) was chosen as the model prison hospice mostly because it is historically one of the worst prisons in the United States, but also, despite its checkered past, Warden Burl Cain had established a hospice worthy of replication throughout the correctional system. At Cain's request, the University Hospital Community Hospice in New Orleans created a program for Angola that met the criteria of the National Hospice and Palliative Care Organization. Services were delivered without additional cost to the prison.

Angola Prison Hospice: Opening the Door, the documentary I made for the conference, introduced this highly successful prison-based hospice program. What made this program exceptional was the decision to train prisoners as hospice volunteers so that they could serve as companions for their dying peers.

Gaining entry into LSP-Angola was relatively simple with the backing of a progressive foundation like OSI, and after the usual background check, I was given considerable freedom to film throughout the infirmary where the prison hospice was being run. Because of the conference deadline I had a 3-week production schedule and had to work 10 to 12 hour days. I spent my evenings off-site at a local motel to rest, repair, and prepare for the next day of shooting.

Since I was producing a promotional video of sorts for LSP-Angola I was met with very little opposition. The medical staff along with the correctional officers who were on-board with the program were willing to be interviewed and readily offered their insights on the fledgling program. The prisoner hospice volunteers, who were a large and unique facet of the hospice program, were overjoyed to praise a program responsible for instilling a pride they had never felt in all their years of incarceration.

Additionally, because the film was about a hospice I also needed to document a terminally ill prisoner who was participating in the hospice program – a difficult situation to film in the free world let alone in a maximum-security prison. I was fortunate to have met a prisoner patient who was amenable to have his final days documented. His visiting family members were also very supportive of the project and of the prison hospice program that allowed them to visit their incarcerated loved-one through his dying days.

Many heartfelt moments of care between the prisoner hospice volunteers and their patients were documented. For most of the prisoners it was the first time they were allowed to offer and accept love and compassion from one another – not a trivial experience for men behind bars.

During my 3-week stay at LSP-Angola I also documented other integral aspects of the hospice program: the Inter-Disciplinary Team (IDT) meetings, the mandatory hospice training classes for security and medical staff, and prospective prisoner hospice volunteers, as well as the bereavement and burial ceremonies.

It should be noted that while most of the medical, security and administrative staff were supportive of the prisoner hospice program, there was also a palpable resentment of the program and of the filmmaker among some of the other staff members. Many of the disgruntled folks asked why additional measures were taken to provide the prisoners with a dignified death when their victims never had that choice. To the dissenters, the hospice program represented a coddling of the prisoner and there was no way the program could ever be justified in their eyes.

As a documentarian, I believe that all aspects of an issue, positive and negative, need to be explored and presented. Consequently I need to be friendly to everyone involved, even those who would rather see me kicked out of the facility!

To soften the shock of having a camera present, when I set out on a verité documentary project, I usually build in a 3 to 4 week period at the beginning to simply get to know the people I am going to film. This period lets the subjects and director build a bond of trust that is critical if we are going to work effectively for an extended period of time. I make observations, ask questions, and answer those the subjects may have about me or the filming process.

In the second phase, I shoot for brief periods throughout the day allowing the subjects to become accustomed to the presence of the camera as well my shooting style. I consider myself to be an "in your face" kind of shooter, so I need my subjects to get used to having the camera a few feet away from their faces or right behind their heads for an intimate over the shoulder shot.

I feel the human face in close-up reveals emotions a medium or long shot simply cannot express. Additionally, since I usually work alone and do not have a sound person with an obtrusive microphone boom pole, I need to be closer to the human voice, in order to clearly record what is being said. And I move in close to the face to capture the telltale emotions. I tend to shoot hand-held instead of being locked-down to a tripod, so I can freely move throughout the scene capturing the action from various angles – mindful of how scenes will fit together in the final editing of the film. Even when conducting a formal interview I tend to hand hold the camera to maintain the organic "hands on" feel I've established with the rest of the footage shot.

While my shooting method may sound intrusive, most people become accustomed to the presence and proximity of the camera especially over an extended period of time. Most of the prisoners I have filmed over the years quickly adapt to having a camera nearby; perhaps because they are constantly under surveillance or rarely have the kind of privacy we have in the free world. Whatever the reason, I have consistently found the prisoner population to be absolutely open to being filmed. The same cannot be said for some of the health care and correctional staff I have filmed over the years. In Angola in particular, some staff members felt obligated to participate in the documentary because it was focusing on a program they had a hand in creating. Despite the dread they had of being interviewed on camera or filmed in action they usually rose to the occasion and performed well. But people are good on camera or they are not, and the latter usually end up on the editing room floor.

Sometimes staff members fear that the camera will "catch them" performing a medical procedure without proper protection, or on duty with their feet up on a desk. These fears must be appeased at the outset in order to build a trusting bond – otherwise a negative and antagonistic atmosphere will develop. If the prison administration grants me permission to enter a facility, it's usually not to create an exposé on the inevitable irregularities of the system.

Meetings with the subjects prior to the production of the documentary are also needed to put people at ease as they learn about how they will be portrayed, where the documentary will be shown, and how much is expected from them during the filmmaking process. I've started projects where I was simply dropped into a location – my reception was far from ideal and took weeks to repair.

While shooting a documentary about the correctional system can be extremely taxing, the feeling of accomplishment when the project is completed and put out into the world always overshadows memories of difficult times. If your film actually causes change to a system in need of transformation – then so much the better. Since the film was released the number of prison hospices that use prisoner volunteers has greatly increased. Now approximately 55 of the 75 known prison hospice programs use prisoner volunteers as hospice workers.

ABOUT THE AUTHOR

Edgar Barens was born in Aurora, Illinois. For the past ten years Barens' documentary work has explored the many issues at play in the American criminal justice system. Before *Prison Terminal,* he directed *Angola Prison Hospice: Opening the Door* and *A Sentence of Their Own, which* chronicles one family's annual pilgrimage to a New Hampshire State Prison, making visible the gradual descent of a family "doing time" on the outside. Barens is producer, director and sometimes editor of his documentary films. He prefers to work solo, believing that a deeper trust is gained with his subjects by working in this manner. Visit http://prisonterminal.com.

RESPONSE

A Symphony in Two Parts:
The JPP and The PEN Prison Writing Program
Susan Nagelsen

As this issue of the *Journal of Prisoners on Prison* goes to press, the United States incarcerates its citizens at a rate six times that of Canada, leading the world in both actual and per capita figures. Rehabilitation has assumed a pejorative connotation, and the continual reduction or elimination of programs is lessening the possibility of being able to effectively prepare prisoners for re-entry to society. In a recent article in *The New York Review of Books*, David Cole (2009, p. 41) succinctly explains this pattern, remarking on the profound lack of empathy for those in prison: "For the vast majority of us ... the idea that we might find ourselves in jail or prison is simply put not a genuine concern".

There are, however, and we are grateful for their presence, men and women who recognize the dysfunctional philosophy that continues to drive the tough-on-crime attitude that has prevailed in the United States for four decades. Bell Chevigny and her colleagues at the PEN America Prison Writing Program have worked tirelessly to remind us of our shared humanity with prisoners and to demonstrate that affinity by showcasing the intellectual and creative products of minds that society has exiled and marginalized to the point of near voicelessness. It is significant that this issue of the *JPP*, edited by Bell Chevigny, appears just as the global recession is forcing retrograde elements in the United States to rethink criminal justice policies that are no longer economically sustainable while the Canadian government continues to move towards increasingly punitive and expensive policy making on prison issues.

The strength of the voices in this issue will not disappoint the reader; the content in the pieces will provide academics and prisoners avenues for discourse whether in the classroom or on the pod. Students will find themselves questioning the wisdom of isolating prisoners in concrete boxes for prolonged periods, while prisoners will nod their heads knowingly. The readers will find humor, even where one might think there should be no joking allowed. In this issue we are regaled with stories that showcase the problems that are prevalent in our prisons today: mental illness, HIV/AIDS, the Three Strikes laws, the violence that permeates these places, and the death penalty. The reader is given insight into the absurdity of living behind the walls, something that the lay person will find interesting and frightening all at once. There are pieces that deal with the continual problems of cultural difference within our institutions of incarceration, and engaging works that offer opportunities for us to rethink the way we view prisons – might we consider them communities? We are asked to ponder the effectiveness of this concept on the rehabilitative nature of the prison complex.

How might the community be able to help is a question we are asked in this issue, and one that is addressed by two different writers. One looks at the affect volunteers can have on the prison community and as a result what the prisoner can then give back to the community upon release. The second looks at programs and partnerships formed with prisons to provide chances for prisoners to enrich their lives through writing, art, and theatre. These programs provide much needed life-altering opportunities for prisoners and volunteers alike, and without programs such as the Prison Creative Arts Project (PCAP) the chance for growth and development might be lost for both parties.

At a time when the Supreme Court of the United States is revisiting current laws that sentence juveniles as young as thirteen to prison for life without parole for non-homicide crimes,[1] the writers in these pages remind us of the contradiction on all human hearts: the urge to punish and the need to forgive. These writers, prisoners and academics alike, urge society to summon the will to accommodate both without denying either.

We must continue the collaboration we have begun, this partnership between scholars, prisoners, and the *JPP* in an environment to facilitate the shifts in policy and philosophy necessary to reform the current system. The authors whose work is featured within these pages, the dedicated scholars and authors who contribute to push the issues of incarceration to the forefront of the discussion all play a vital role in the battle to work for change. Without the dedication and intervention of scholars, authors and volunteers like those associated with the PEN Prison Writing Program, without the commitment and perseverance of journals like the *JPP*, and without the courage and determination of the incarcerated writers featured here, those on the outside working for change would be in danger of what the ancient Greeks warned us about 2500 years ago: "The worst and final temptation... is to stop the fight [against injustice] and slide into inactivity of heart and will" (Roche, 1962, p. xvii).

Apathy in the face of injustice is not an option. To force a system to change one must throw back the curtains and allow the light to pour into the room illuminating the dirt and the cobwebs as well as the places in the corners where the filth can hide. These writers, this journal, and the volunteers who keep the PEN Prison Writing Program alive and well teach this lesson as few can.

ENDNOTES

[1] *Johnson v. Florida.* Oral arguments before the Court were heard on November 9, 2009.

REFERENCES

Cole, David (2009) "Can our Shameful Prisons Be Reformed?", *The New York Review of Books*, page 41 – November 9.

Roche, Paul (ed.) (1962) "Introduction", in *The Orestes Plays of Aeschylus*, New American Library of Canada.

ABOUT THE AUTHOR

Susan Nagelsen is Director of the Writing Program at New England College in Henniker, New Hampshire, where she has taught for twenty-four years. She is an essayist and a fiction writer as well as the author of two writing manuals. She teaches first-year courses as well as advanced essay writing courses such as the art of the essay and content based writing. She also teaches in the Criminal Justice program where her course focuses on teaching students about prison from the point of view of prisoners. Her most recent published fiction can be found in the fall 2005 edition of the *Henniker Review*, *Tacenda*, *Bleakhouse Review* and in the *Journal of Prisoners on Prison* Volume 14(2), an issue addressing aging in prison. She is a frequent contributor to the *JPP* and is currently Associate Editor. She is also the editor of an anthology of work by incarcerated writers entitled *Exiled Voices, Portals of Discovery* (New England College Press, 2008). The book features 13 incarcerated writers with an introduction to each written by Nagelsen and is being used as a textbook in courses focusing on criminal justice issues.

Stepping from One State of Mind into a New One
Drake Stutesman

This interesting group of non-fiction pieces raises many important points about prison but, as much, they show the essential role that writing does and can play in prison life. Writing is crucial to our society, of course, but, as a teacher in prison, I found that the part it plays there has many special qualities. I teach creative writing and literature in university and in community colleges. I taught creative writing for three years in London's HMP Holloway, the largest women's prison in Europe, holding about 600 people. The median age of the prisoners was 22 years old. A few were as young as 16. Holloway is a remand unit so the population was always in transition. Some prisoners were awaiting trial and were there for only months while others were serving very long sentences and were there for years before being rotated out.

My classes were never stable, as students could return week after week but new students could join every day, thus precluding a consistent group. The group's abilities were extremely variable. My students included women who could barely read and write and others who were highly educated; in one instance, I had a woman with a Ph.D in linguistics from a top London university. Students came to these classes for different reasons: some to learn, some to get money, meet a friend or make a contact. Many were very angry or very subdued, some were mentally ill (and should not have been in prison), and some were calm and attentive. Students could be high, frightened or bored. Though prison is often perceived as a place where one has "lots of time", therefore writing is easy, my experience was that this is not true. Prison is filled with intense distraction: it is very loud (there is much yelling), nerve wracking, enervating, depressing, and pressurizing. It also is not comfortable to open up in prison... exposing personal feelings can bring ridicule, violence or a sense of dangerous vulnerability. That anyone in prison could write *anything,* much less anything good, was always a phenomenon to me. But despite these volatilities, an astounding energy and a talent emerged from the restless women in the Holloway classroom.

I found that the prison students responded to class exercises in ways that I experienced nowhere else. This showed in their attitudes toward writing, in their talent, in their imagination and their need to express. I tried to teach Creative Writing as a way to experiment with words and to reveal to students what words could do. I hoped they could open to the realization that there are many ways to write down one's experiences, as opposed to simply writing them without understanding the power of expression itself. I put less emphasis on confessional pieces than on exercises that asked for inventive word play or exploring fun topics.

I discovered that there was a qualitative difference between prison students and students on the outside. The prisoners were more intrepid and more imaginative. In the classes outside prison, students often were insecure. They hesitated and were circumspect in taking a leap. The students at Holloway jumped in immediately and often came up with extravagant, entertaining, off beat pieces. I still remember some of their wonderful adjectives, phrases or plotlines or the cleverness of words used in a nonsense sestina or in evocative rhymes.

This is only one slice of the uniqueness of what writing does in prison. This journal's collection covers much of the breadth of writing's value there. Marilyn Buck is attentive to the nature of language itself. She wonders how we think about it, how it forms our identities, our thoughts, and how we are dominated by it. She sees the argument that language enforces class structures as especially exacerbated in prison where any kind of refusal to conform can be lethal. Jorge Antonio Renaud recognizes writing's bottom line as being a forum in which to "express frustration with prison's rigid code" and Buzz Alexander, who initiated the Prison Creative Arts Project, sees it similarly, but from a different perspective. After a series of refusals, he realized that *articulating* a program's worth to a director was as essential a route to getting a mandate as having a worthwhile curriculum. Judith Clark uses the essay form to examine the U.S. government's draconian cut backs to penal education in the 1990s and the disastrous effect that not having a place to express had on the system. Patricia Prewitt shows just how valuable expression is in her painful, humorous vent about the anomalous rules that a prisoner navigates even in buying from the canteen or creating something in art class. Charles Norman, Michael Rothwell and G.T. Carrillo, vividly describe the futility that prisoners often feel and how many have given up because they see no way to cope with their intense feelings.

Articulation begins all education. In prison, words act as outreach to an uninformed society, as solidarity with those who empathize, or as a route to self-acceptance. This is not atypical of writing in general and all these elements of expression, understanding, and communication are part of any teaching. But the complexities, raw feeling and potential for release from pain or release from ignorance are a hundred fold in any part of teaching, writing, and learning in prison. Political prisoners have often spoken of the need to write, of the solace that it gives them and how it soothes or expresses the world within a world that they inhabit in order to cope with prison, imprisonment and the prison organization. More than one prisoner has described how writing for a PEN contest or how learning to write expressively has meant stepping from one state of mind into an entirely new one. Writing, from reform proposals to a first poem, is one of prison's most vibrant, most enduring and most necessary lifelines.

ABOUT THE AUTHOR

Drake Stutesman has taught courses in literature and cinema at New York University, Montclair University, the School of Visual Arts, and the University of North London (UK). She has been a member of PEN's Prison Writing Committee since 2001 and is the Co-Chair of *The Women's Film Preservation Fund*. She is a novelist and the author of the cultural history *Snake* (Reaktion Press, 2005). Her work has been published by, among others, the British Film Institute, MoMA, Koenig Books, University of Illinois Press, Gale Press, *Bookforum,* and *Film Quarterly.* She edits *Framework: the Journal of Cinema and Media.*

PRISONERS' STRUGGLES

The Battle for Felon Re-enfranchisement
Bruce Reilly

"Hi, howya doing? My name's Bruce and I'm going around telling folks about Question 2 on the ballot this year. Have you heard about Question 2? No? Well, we're trying to get voting rights back for people convicted of crimes who are out here living in the community. They're out here raising kids, working jobs just like anybody else, and we want them more involved rather than pushed aside and demonized. Tossing people into shadows, not letting them get work, or have a voice... that's just likely to cause more drug use, more crimes, and that's not the kind of society we want to live in. So whaddya think about that?"

And so it went, leading up to the 2006 elections. I was in a unique position: a full-time student – living off loans and a campus job – on a mini-tour of my play, *Voice of the Voiceless*, while also taking on this major ballot initiative. I was just a year out of prison. One can only volunteer to do so much activism, so thankfully the Brennan Center, JEHT Foundation, and others made funding possible to hire a staff. With 35 states disenfranchising 5.3 million citizens, as of 2009, we need to liberate entire state populations. The numbers rise so fast in this field, our T-shirts from 2005 had to raise the number of disenfranchised in Rhode Island by 4000 in 2006.

It was do or die to change the constitution. My good friend Andres was a new student at Brown University. He served as one of our first X-cons to prove who it is the people were fighting for, acting as a spokesman. I encouraged him to focus on his studies. He encouraged me to work with the coordinated Campaign in the pursuit of concrete reform. I didn't take the job to be a poster child, nor did anyone want me in that role, so I started to advocate and organize.

My task was to recruit and train the volunteers for canvassing the neighborhoods. From colleges to X-cons to churches, I wanted to be everywhere at once. My play was itself a recruiting, informational, and a PR tool. It was exciting going door-to-door and helping people figure out an opinion on the matter. For the first time, I realized *people are good.* We hit up the rich and poor, Black, White, Latino – it is amazing how easy a personal conversation can dispel the myths about prisoners.

Although our campaign ultimately included the collective efforts of about 1000 people, our core staff was less than 10 people. Imagine: a handful of people changed the constitution of Rhode Island by influencing 52 percent of the state. We concentrated our efforts in the six cities, where we won by 18,000 votes. We relied on media alone in the 33 other districts, and lost by 7,000. I attribute much of the credit to my friend Dan Schleifer, the Field Coordinator – and effectively, Executive Director – for our Voting Rights campaign.

Following the passage of Question 2, I became perhaps the first parolee to register to vote in the history of Rhode Island, and I spoke to a young legislator at the forefront of social justice issues. I asked what progressive proposals we should be on the lookout for, and he replied, "What bills would *you* like to see?" I was stunned. To my knowledge, nobody had ever asked a prisoner what legislative changes we should make in Rhode Island. Being on parole, by the way, is still serving a prison sentence – just doing it "at liberty". While Maine and Vermont are the only states that never took away the right to vote, even while in prison, ten states allow for some people to be permanently disenfranchised, with Florida, Kentucky and Virginia's being practically absolute. Leaders should be asking some of these thousands about *their* take on reforming the system.

I explained to Representative David Segal that if you go into the prison, people talk about one issue: Probation Violation. When 30,000 Rhode Islanders are on probation, particularly young men of color, we have a fish in the barrel situation. Accusations are dealt with through arrest and imprisonment, with low standards of proof to declare someone a "violator" and subjected to long imprisonments. If you break it down to two major unjust components: (1) we are Violated before the new accusation is dealt with, and there is no mechanism to "undo" the Violation when one is later absolved on the accusation; and (2) if someone gets in trouble with a day left on their 10 year Probation, they can be sentenced to the entire 10 years in prison. These result in tremendous leverage, creating a system where 98 percent of convictions are from guilty pleas, eliminating trials, whether one is innocent of the new charges or not. Segal asked me to write up the bills, and my legal research provided the basis and case – of my friend Rich – to blow the roof off this issue.

Most don't know, but I'll share it here: I was fired from the Right to Vote Campaign in a dispute about whether I could reveal my status as a paroled murderer. Dan explained to higher ups that he wasn't sure we could win without me, that they'd cut off his right arm, as he put it. That feeling of being a valuable asset is how I felt in prison, so it's quite something for anyone to come out and hear you aren't needed. I was a Jailhouse Lawyer, the resident artist, and someone always needed the services I spent years developing. I organized the sports and game tournaments, and served as a voice of reason when it came to violence or race relations. Prison is a meritocracy, not the elitist class system America protects. The firing lasted a week, but the memory lasts forever.

Rehabilitation and Re-Entry are another front in the prison-industrial complex (PIC). A front that is "Defending the Guilty" – as my friend Bell put it simply. This is the only human rights movement in history to be defending the guilty, which indicates just how far we've gone beyond "punishment" until it resembles oppression. Whereas most of my brethren and I are guilty, we need to know that our allies are actually defending and truly respecting us. Furthermore, we need to be needed, not just for our collective self-esteem, but more so that genuine solutions can be achieved.

The social engineers and activist organizations have very few X-Cons in decision-making roles. It is disrespectful to tell a 35-year-old man, who has studied for a decade in prison, to spend $100,000 to study alongside teenagers for a piece of paper. Particularly when a man has the System pressuring him to stay employed, has children to feed, and owns nothing but the clothes on his back and the contents of his mind. Such a man needs to be a resource, and needs the role models of those who came before him.

Rhode Island is now among 14 states that restore rights upon release from prison. The bulk of states require a completion of parole AND probation – which can take decades – with seven states maintaining financial requirements – court fees, child support, and so on – to vote. In May 2009, Washington eliminated these payments, thereby becoming the twentieth state in the past ten years to ease voting restrictions. Senator Russ Feingold (D-WI) and Representative John Conyers (D-MI) introduced the Democracy Restoration Act (DRA) last year. The DRA would re-enfranchise nearly four million people who have been released from prison.

Structural reforms are what stoke my fire, and The Right to Vote Campaign became a gateway drug to systemic change. The people we activated, the popular conceptions, and the legislative mentality have given us momentum to gain passage of Probation Reform and ending Mandatory Minimums. The Governor vetoed both, but the power shift has already begun.

ABOUT THE AUTHOR

Bruce Reilly is an artist, writer, and activist in Providence, Rhode Island. In 2005, he published *NewJack's Guide to the Big House* (1000 lbs. Gorilla Media), "the treatise of a ghetto philosopher". "As a Man who is now 'free'", he writes, "I can tell you that all my work in prison pays off triple on the Outside". He is a Board member of Direct Action for Rights and Equality, and his latest project is a documentary on a private prison in Central Falls, Rhode Island. He, Andres, and thousands of others cast their first ballot in 2008. Andres is currently a student at Yale University Law School.

My Journey to Reform the Rockefeller Drug Laws
Anthony Papa

On April 24, 2009, I attended an historic bill-signing ceremony that hammered another nail into the coffin of the Rockefeller Drug Laws. In Corona, Queens, at the Elmcor Community Center, Governor Paterson signed the document to put into place the reforms that activists like me had sought for thirty-six years. Standing tall at a podium, Patterson said, "For years, thousands of New Yorkers have spoken out against the Rockefeller Drug Laws... This is a proud day for me and so many of my colleagues who have fought for so long to overhaul the drug laws and restore judicial discretion in narcotics cases".

The Rockefeller Drug Laws were enacted in 1973 by the New York State Legislature to satisfy Governor Nelson Rockefeller's attempt to curb the drug epidemic of that time. Harsh mandatory minimum sentences were imposed on those caught selling two ounces or possessing 4 ounces of a controlled substance. Instead of satisfying the legislative intent of locking up major kingpins and curbing the epidemic, it did the opposite, putting first time non-violent offenders away for sentences of 15 years to life. Locking up Blacks and Latinos at alarming rates had a drastic effect on communities of color, and caused the New York's State's prison system to burst at its seams.

The new bill not only restored judicial discretion in most drug cases, but also expanded alternatives to incarceration and invested millions in treatment. Activists like Gabriel Sayegh, project director with the Drug Policy Alliance said, "Governor Paterson has helped to move our state in a new direction on drug policy, one based on public health and safety, in fairness and justice. This shows what is possible when people come together and work for change". While advocates applaud the changes, they also point out that reforms should have gone even further. For instance, some mandatory minimum sentences for drug offenses still remain intact, and harsh penalties for low-level drug offenses remain on the books.

This day was a total vindication for me, because in 1985 I was given a 15-years-to-life sentence for a first time non-violent drug offense. Nothing in the world could have prepared me for life in the gulag. I was sent to Sing Sing, a maximum security prison in Ossining, New York. It was a living nightmare. Not only did I lose my family, I lost my life as I knew it. When I arrived at the prison, I was surrounded by a sea of faces of men who had lost all faith in their lives. It was the lowest point in my life.

Soon after, I was walking past a row of cells on the top tier of the A Block housing unit. I smelled paint and followed its trail to a cell. I looked in and saw the most magnificent paintings They belonged to a prisoner named Indio. We became friends and he taught me how to paint.

I became absorbed in my art. I was hooked. In 1988, I was sitting in my cell and picked up a mirror. I saw a man who was going to be spending the most productive years of his life locked in a cage. I set up a canvas and captured the image, which I named "15 to Life". In 1994 this self-portrait was exhibited at the Whitney Museum of American Art where it received a lot of media attention. In 1997, after 12 years in prison, I received executive clemency from Governor George Pataki. Upon release I began having exhibits and used my art as an instrument to speak out against inhumane drug laws.

At the same time I traveled to Albany to speak with legislators, most of whom had a dual view of reforming the laws. Their public view was that the Rockefeller Drug Laws were working fine, but behind closed doors they agreed that they needed to be reformed. They were afraid of speaking out against them, because it would cause their political deaths.

To try to change the way politicians thought about New York's drug laws, we had to change their constituents' views. In 1998, I co-founded the Mothers of the New York Disappeared. The group was modeled on their Argentinean counterparts. The Madres of the Plaza de Mayo have marched weekly since the 1970s in front of the Casa Rosada (the Presidential palace), bearing photos of their children and grandchildren "disappeared" during the military dictatorship.

In 1997, we passed out flyers at a bus terminal to family members that took buses up to New York State prisons and requested those who had loved ones imprisoned by the Rockefeller Drug Laws to join our group. The request was looked upon by some as a blessing because they wanted to help change the laws that imprisoned many of their relatives. On May 8, 1998, about 25 family members of people imprisoned by the Drug Laws demonstrated at Rockefeller Center at 50th Street and Fifth Avenue in NYC. Putting faces on those who were "doing time outside" generated a lot of press.

Several years later the media had a field day when a delegation of Madres – one of them now seventy-eight – flew from Buenos Aires, wearing their emblematic white scarves, to join the New York Mothers at a press conference on the steps of City Hall to protest the Rockefeller Drug Laws.

We made a trip to Albany New York where they met with members of the New York Assembly and Senate. Robert Morganthau, the New York City District Attorney, was so impressed with them he gave them a private tour of his NYC office and did a photo shoot with the Madres.

It was a long row to hoe, but we eventually shifted public opinion, which then put pressure on the politicians. In 2004-2005, we got the first changes in the law, but they were watered-down, and activists like myself were not satisfied and pushed for further reform. Even these changes did not come easily because of the New York State legislature's reluctance to tamper with the quagmire created by Governor Nelson Rockefeller in 1973.

Some had considered the Rockefeller Laws the answer to the so-called drug epidemic. But the harsh sentencing guidelines with their mandatory minimums did nothing more than fuel the prison-industrial complex and give relief to economically depressed rural upstate communities by incarcerating low level non-violent drug offenders. The Rockefeller Laws also led to the building of thirty-eight prisons since 1982, mostly in Republican senate districts, at an operating cost of over a billion dollars annually. Seen as a cash cow for these upstate rural districts, the Rockefeller Laws became an untouchable political issue

Joining upstate politicians were prosecutors who became staunch opponents of any Rockefeller reform legislation. They used the Laws as a powerful prosecutorial tool, claiming to shield society from harm associated with drugs and addiction. But in reality the only effect of the Laws was massive incarceration for hundreds of thousands of low level non-violent drug offenders, who should have had treatment instead. Of these, over 90 percent were Black and Latino. The Rockefeller Drug Laws generated a racist entity that completely failed to balance justice and protection of our communities.

With perseverance and determination we fought for meaningful reform for thirty-six years, and this year we achieved it. Following the new reforms President Obama's new drug czar, former Seattle Police Chief Gil Kerlikowske called for an end to the war on drugs and said we are not at war with people in this country.

I agree. Now it's time to embrace the New Rockefeller Reforms and set free those who received harsh mandatory sentencing and who are eligible for judicial relief, so they may be reunited with their families and start productive lives as citizens of New York.

ABOUT THE AUTHOR

Anthony Papa is an artist, writer, noted advocate against the war on drugs and co-founder of the Mothers of the New York Disappeared. His opinion pieces about the drug war have appeared in the *Huffington Post*, among others. He is a public speaker and college lecturer on art and on criminal justice issues. Currently, he is a communications specialist for Drug Policy Alliance in NYC. Papa is the author of *15 to Life: How I Painted My Way to Freedom* (Feral House, 2004), a memoir about his experience of being sentenced to state prison for a first-time, non-violent drug offense under New York's draconian Rockefeller Drug Laws. *The New York Times, The Washington Post, The Nation,* National Public Radio, "Democracy Now", Court TV, "Extra", and C-Span have interviewed him. Papa has appeared on nationally syndicated talk shows such as "Charles Grodin", "Geraldo Rivera", and "Catherine Crier Live". His art has been exhibited at the Whitney Museum of American Art in New York as well as other venues.

The Coalition of Women Prisoners
Tamar Kraft-Stolar

The Coalition for Women Prisoners[1] is an alliance of individuals and organizations in New York State dedicated to making the criminal justice system more responsive to the needs and rights of women and their families. The Coalition is coordinated by the Women in Prison Project of the Correctional Association of New York (CA), a non-profit criminal justice policy organization. One of four initiatives at the CA, the Women in Prison Project works to stop the misuse of incarceration as a response to the social ills that drive crime, to make prison conditions for women humane and just, and to create a criminal justice system that addresses women's specific needs and that treats people and their families with fairness, dignity, and respect. In 1846, the New York State Legislature granted the CA authority to inspect prisons and report its findings. The CA is the only organization in New York State – and one of only two in the country – with this statutory authority. Under the CA's legislative mandate, the Women in Prison Project monitors conditions inside correctional facilities that house women in New York. The Project also manages ReConnect, an advocacy and leadership training program for women recently released from prison and jail.

In 1994, the Project formed the Coalition for Women Prisoners in response to the rising numbers of women in prison, and with the recognition that issues facing women in the criminal justice system require specific attention and advocacy. From 1973 to 2009, New York's total prison population increased nearly 388 percent – its female prison population rose more than 580 percent.[2]

The Coalition now includes over 1,300 individuals from more than 100 organizations across the state. Membership is composed of formerly incarcerated people, social service providers, academics, attorneys, city as well as state agency staff, non-profit organizations, faith and community leaders, and concerned individuals.

The Coalition's goals are to: ensure that criminal justice policy is fair, humane, and reflective of the specific issues facing women; improve conditions in women's prisons; protect incarcerated mothers' ability to maintain bonds with and rights to their children; remove barriers to re-entry and allow women to make a safe and productive return to their communities; educate the public and policymakers about key criminal justice issues affecting women and families; facilitate formerly incarcerated women's leadership in efforts to change policies that directly affect their lives; and, ensure that currently and formerly incarcerated women's voices and perspectives are included in the larger pubic debate around criminal justice reform.

The Coalition also aims to reduce the stigma associated with currently and formerly incarcerated women, and to build recognition that "behind every label is a woman with a story"[3] – that women should not be defined solely by their crimes, absent an understanding of the various circumstances that affect their lives and actions. Central to the Coalition's work is the belief that, instead of spending vast sums on incarceration, government officials should expand the funding for and use of gender-specific, community-based alternatives to incarceration. These programs increase community health and safety, save taxpayers money, and give people the opportunities they need to rebuild their lives and families, and to contribute meaningfully to society.

To achieve its goals, the Coalition engages in a variety of tactics and strategies, including legislative and policy advocacy, lobbying, research and policy analysis, public education, community organizing, and media work. Recent accomplishments include:

1) Successfully advocating for the passage of three bills: one that bans the use of shackles and restraints on incarcerated women during labor, childbirth and post-delivery recovery in New York's prisons and jails; another that requires the State Department of Health to monitor HIV and hepatitis C care in New York's prisons and jails;[4] and a third that requires New York to suspend, instead of terminate, Medicaid for people entering prison and jail with prior Medicaid enrollment.[5]

2) Securing funding for a Family Reunion Program at Albion Correctional Facility. Albion, the largest prison for women in New York, is eight hours from New York City, making it difficult for many incarcerated mothers to stay connected with their children.[6] The program, which allows mothers overnight visits in trailers on the facility's property, can help lessen the harsh effects of incarceration on families and ease reunification after prison.

3) Publishing a unique re-entry guide, *My Sister's Keeper*, which highlights formerly incarcerated women's voices and allows women coming home to learn from the life experiences of others who have been through a similar process.

4) Establishing a women's health section composed of 50 books and 100 pamphlets, in the general libraries of each women's prison, and established a parent and family resource section in the general libraries and children's centers.
5) Organizing the Coalition's 15th annual Advocacy Day, bringing 200 formerly incarcerated women and other advocates to Albany to discuss key issues affecting women in the criminal justice system with more than 100 state legislators.

The Coalition's three Committees – Incarcerated Mothers, Conditions/Re-entry, and Violence Against Women – meet every month and drive the Coalition's policy agenda. Although the Women in Prison Project staffs the Coalition, membership is diverse and each Committee is led by members from different organizations. Monthly Coalition and Committee meetings are open to all individuals interested in making change in the criminal justice system for women and families.

The Incarcerated Mothers Committee focuses on helping mothers in prison and their children maintain bonds and relationships – often in jeopardy of being shattered as a result of incarceration. Almost 73 percent of women in New York's prisons are parents, compared to 58 percent of men.[7] More than 10,000 children have a mother in a jail or prison in New York State.[8] Over 77 percent of mothers in state prison nationwide were their children's primary caretakers before arrest, compared with about 26 percent of men.[9]

The Committee's current legislative priority is the Adoption and Safe Families Act (ASFA) Expanded Discretion Bill. ASFA – a federal law enacted in 1997 – almost always requires foster care agencies to file termination of parental rights papers if a child has been in foster care for 15 of the last 22 months.[10] Although ASFA does have limited exceptions, they are rarely employed in cases involving incarcerated parents. Ultimately, ASFA's timeframe puts incarcerated parents at disproportionate risk of losing rights to their children forever. The ASFA Expanded Discretion Bill would grant foster care agencies discretion to delay filing termination papers after 15 months when a parent is incarcerated yet continues to play a meaningful role in the child's life. The bill would also amend New York's child welfare laws to reflect the special circumstances and needs of families separated by incarceration. As part of its campaign for the bill, the Committee created a short film, *A Fair Chance*, featuring two formerly incarcerated mothers whose parental rights were terminated and one young boy whose mother lost her rights to him while she was in prison.

The Violence Against Women Committee focuses on changing the criminal justice system's response to survivors of domestic violence and abuse. Domestic violence and women's pathways to prison are inextricably linked: 82 percent of women at New York's Bedford Hills Correctional Facility report having a childhood history of severe physical and/or sexual abuse and 75 percent report having experienced violence by an intimate partner during adulthood.[11] Nationwide, more than 57 percent of women in state prisons and 55 percent in local jails report having been physically or sexually abused in the past.[12]

Domestic violence survivors of abuse who defend themselves or commit other crimes as a result of abuse are often sent to prison for long periods of time with little chance to earn early release. To help address this issue, the Committee is drafting a legislative proposal that would expand judicial discretion and allow judges the option of sending survivors to alternative-to-incarceration programs, reduce sentence lengths for survivors, and reform sentencing laws to allow incarcerated survivors to petition the courts to review their sentences and consider granting early release from prison. The Committee is also using its 20-minute documentary, *Strength of a Woman*, to educate policymakers as well as the public about the intersection of domestic violence and women's incarceration.

The Conditions and Re-entry Committee focuses on improving conditions inside prison and eliminating barriers facing women when they return home. About 2,600 women are incarcerated in New York's prisons, 4.3 percent of the state's total prison population.[13] More than 27,260 people were released from state prison in 2008 – 1,855 of whom were women.[14]

The Committee's main legislative goal is to secure adequate funding for a bill it recently helped pass which requires the State Department of Health to monitor HIV/AIDS and hepatitis C care in New York's prisons and jails. More than 12 percent of women in New York's prisons are HIV positive – a rate of infection more than double the rate for male prisoners and 80 times higher than the rate in the general public.[15] Just over 22 percent of women in New York's prisons have hepatitis C, a rate of infection almost double the rate for men in prison[16] and more than 14 times higher than the rate in the general public.[17] Until the passage of this bill, the Department of Health

– the only government agency in New York with a statutory mandate to monitor pubic health services – played no role in monitoring the quality of health services in prison. This bill is a positive step toward the Committee's long-term goal of requiring the Department of Health to oversee all health care services in New York's prisons.

The Committee is also working to expand access to affordable housing for women transitioning home. To this end, the Committee is creating a peer-based guide to help women navigate the process of securing housing after release and preparing to draft legislation that protects individuals with felony convictions from discrimination in securing housing.

The Coalition for Women Prisoners represents a useful model for collective advocacy: members' diverse viewpoints, experiences and skills inform and shape the Coalition's agenda, allow the group to employ a broad range of strategies to affect systemic change, and strengthen the effort to convince policy makers to adopt critical criminal justice reforms. Coalitions can serve as an important vehicle to facilitate the active participation and leadership of individuals directly affected by policies the group seeks to change. They can be a critical part not only of changing policy but also of changing the power-dynamics of policy making itself.

ENDNOTES

[1] There is another and unrelated California Coalition for Women Prisoners (CCWP). From http://womenprisoners.org: "CCWP is a grassroots social justice organization, with members inside and outside prison, that challenges the institutional violence imposed on women, transgender people, and communities of color by the prison industrial complex (PIC). We see the struggle for racial and gender justice as central to dismantling the PIC and we prioritize the leadership of the people, families, and communities most impacted in building this movement."

[2] Figures derived from *Daily Population Capacity Report, 01/01/09,* New York State Department of Correctional Services (NYS DOCS). Letter from NYS DOCS Director of Public Information, 5/15/01. Since 1999, New York's total prison population dropped by almost 15 percent and the state's female prison population fell by more than 25 percent. Notwithstanding this positive trend, there are still far too many people under criminal justice supervision in New York: as of January 2009, the state's prison population was just under 61,000 – more than 2,600 (4.3 percent) were women. Almost 31,500 people were on parole, nearly 2,580 (8 percent) of whom were women, and over 122,150 people were on probation, just over 24,080 (20 percent) of whom were women. *See Daily Population Capacity Report, 01/01/09; Hub System: Profile of Inmate Population Under Custody on January 1, 2000,* NYS

DOCS at 2; *Male and Female Parolees in Intensive and Regular Supervision Status by Self Reported Race as of 12/31/08*, New York State Division of Parole; *Total Probationers Supervised Statewide 1/1/2009*, New York State Division of Probation and Correctional Alternatives.

[3]　See Kathy Boudin and Rosyln D. Smith, "Women in Prison: Alive Behind the Labels", in *Sisterhood Is Forever: The Women's Anthology for a New Millenium,* Robin Morgan (ed.), 2003.

[4]　Previous to this bill, health facilities in New York's prisons and jails were the only substantial public health institutions in the state exempt from mandatory, independent assessments by the Department of Health.

[5]　Under previous policy, individuals would commonly have to wait 45 to 90 days after release to receive Medicaid.

[6]　Nearly 41 percent of New York's incarcerated women are housed in Albion Correctional Facility, eight hours away from Manhattan. About 55 percent of the state's female prison population comes from, and will likely return to, the New York City area. Figures derived from *Daily Population Capacity Report, 01/01/09* and *Hub System: Profile of Inmate Population Under Custody on January 1, 2008*, NYS DOCS (March 2008) at 10.

[7]　Letter from NYS DOCS Commissioner Brian Fischer, 3/26/09, on file with Correctional Association of New York.

[8]　*Id.* Jail figures estimated based on data reported from women under DOCS custody.

[9]　See Lauren E. Glaze and Laura M. Maruschak, *Parents in Prison and Their Minor Children* (August 2008, rev 1/8/09), at 16.

[10]　For federal ASFA law, *see*: Public Law 105-89, codified at 42 U.S.C. §§ 670 – 679a. New York's ASFA laws codified in sections of the State's Social Services and Domestic Relations Law, and Family Court Act, *see* N.Y. Soc. Serv. L. § 384-b.

[11]　See A. Browne, B. Miller and E. Maguin, "Prevalence and Severity of Lifetime Physical and Sexual Victimization Among Incarcerated Women", *International Journal of Law & Psychiatry* 22(3-4) (1999).

[12]　See *Prior Abuse Reported by Inmates and Probationers*, Bureau of Justice Statistics, U.S. Department of Justice (April 1999), at 2 and Doris J. James, *Profile of Jail Inmates, 2002*, Bureau of Justice Statistics, U.S. Department of Justice (July 2004), at 10.

[13]　As of January 2009, 60,931 people were under DOCS custody in New York State; 59,823 were men. *Daily Population Capacity Report, 01/01/09.* New York has the fourth largest prison population, exceeded by California, Texas and Florida, respectively. Heather C. West and William J. Sabol, *Prison Inmates at Midyear 2008 – Statistical Tables*, Bureau of Justice Statistics, U.S. Department of Justice (March 2009), at 3. New York has the ninth largest population of incarcerated women in the U.S., exceeded by Texas, California, Florida, Ohio, Arizona, Georgia, Virginia and Illinois, respectively. *Prison Inmates at Midyear 2008*, at 5. From 1973 to 2009, the number of women in New York's prisons increased by more than 580 percent. During the same time period, the state's total prison population increased by nearly 388 percent. Figures derived from *Daily Population Capacity Report, 01/01/09* Letter from DOCS Director of Public Information, 5/15/01.

14   Figures derived from Table 9A (Releases by Crime, Men Only) Crime by Race by Release Type by Release Type; All Releases from NYSDOCS in 2008 Due to Parole, Conditional Release or Maximum Expiration of Sentence, and Table 9B (Releases by Crime, Women Only) Crime by Race by Release Type by Release Type; All Releases from NYSDOCS in 2008 Due to Parole, Conditional Release or Maximum Expiration of Sentence, NYS DOCS.

15   Laura M. Maruschak, *HIV in Prisons, 2005*, Bureau of Justice Statistics, U.S. Department of Justice (September 2007, revised 12/20/07). *See Table 1: Annual Estimates of the Population for the United States and States, and for Puerto Rico: April 1, 2000 to July 1, 2005*, U.S. Census Bureau (2005) and *HIV Infection and AIDS: An Overview*, U.S. Department of Health and Human Services, National Institute of Allergy and Infectious Diseases (NIAID) (March 2005).

16   *Healthcare in New York State Prisons, 2004-2007*, Prison Visiting Project of the Correctional Association of New York (January 2009). Authors of this study calculated these figures by using data from the New York State Department of Health's blind Hepatitis seroprevalence tests of newly admitted inmates to state custody conducted every two years since 2001. Authors applied this data to the number of inmates entering state custody in 2006. A State Department of Health seroprevalence study of 4,000 inmates admitted to DOCS custody from September 2000 to March 2001 found that 23.1 percent of female inmates and 13.6 percent of male inmates were infected with HCV. L. Smith, L. Wang, L. Wright, K. Sabin, D. Glebatis and P. Smith, *Hepatitis C Virus (HCV) Seroprevalence Among Incoming Inmates in New York State (NYS) 2000-2001*, Presented at the Infectious Disease Society of America Meeting 10/24-27/02, Chicago, IL (Poster #793).

17   Gregory L. Armstrong, Annemarie Wasley, Edgar P. Simard, Geraldine M. McQuillan, Wendi L. Kuhnert, and Miriam J. Alter, *The Prevalence of Hepatitis C Virus Infection in the United States, 1999 through 2002*, Annals of Internal Medicine, Volume 144, Number 10705 (May 16, 2006), at 707. *See* "Viral Hepatitis C Fact Sheet", National Center for HIV, STD & TB Prevention, Centers for Disease Control and Prevention (May 24, 2005).

ABOUT THE AUTHOR

Tamar Kraft-Stolar has been the Director of the Women in Prison Project at the Correctional Association of New York (CA) since 2003. In her position, Ms. Kraft-Stolar leads prison monitoring visits, manages coalition and policy advocacy work, drafts legislation and policy materials, and supervises all other aspects of the Project's work. She is co-author of the CA's report, *When "Free" Means Losing Your Mother: The Collision of Child Welfare and the Incarceration of Women in New York State*. Previously, Ms. Kraft-Stolar worked for the CA's Public Policy Project, coordinating its statewide campaign to repeal New York's mandatory minimum drug laws (see www.correctionalassociation.com/WIPP/cwp.htm*)*.

Reflections on 4strugglemag
and the Importance of Media Projects with Prisoners
Sara Falconer, Karen Emily Suurtamm and Jaan Laaman

4strugglemag (see www.4strugglemag.org) is a print and online magazine edited by anti-imperialist political prisoner Jaan Karl Laaman, who is currently imprisoned in USP Tucson, Arizona. It is produced, printed and distributed with the help of members of the Toronto Anarchist Black Cross Federation (ABCF). As a collaborative initiative, it is a work-in-progress, constantly evolving and gaining strength as our community grows.

The idea for the project took root in 2002, when Laaman expressed a desire to develop a publication that gave voice to political prisoners – where they could share their insights, not just about "prison issues", but about current world issues, struggles and events. By early 2004, we had produced our first issue and this year we released Issue 14.

There are more than 100 political prisoners and prisoners of war (PP/POWs) in the United States, coming from the Black Power, Puerto Rican, Asian, indigenous, white anti-imperialist, anarchist and anti-authoritarian movements. Many PP/POWs were active in the civil rights movements of the 1960s and 1970s and have already spent more than 30 years in prison. And now, with the renewed criminalization of dissent, more and more activists, particularly from animal rights and environmental movements, are facing jail time. In order to continue their activism and advocacy for social justice, these prisoners rely on the support of the larger activist community, which benefits in turn from their continued participation.

THE IMPORTANCE OF MEDIA PROJECTS WITH PRISONERS

You do not have to support political prisoners, advocate for human rights for prisoners overall, or subscribe to a particularly radical ideology in order to recognize the importance of media projects with prisoners. The issue at stake is the right to communicate. Prisons are a form of censorship, silencing the voices of millions.

As Michel Foucault (1977) notes in *Discipline and Punish*, the rise of industrial capitalism in the eighteenth century was accompanied by the rise of the modern prison. Corporal punishment was increasingly replaced by confinement as the object of penal repression moved from the body to the mind. In *Prison Life and Human Worth*, Paul W. Keve (1974) notes that prisoners are allowed to communicate, but only in a highly regulated and formal exchange of information, which deprives them of a large part of human communication. He suggests that the need for human communication is so basic that it escapes notice, even though it is actually essential to interpersonal relationships and psychological health: "Personality health requirements so basic as these cannot be tampered with except at serious risk. Sooner or later the prisoner must lose his spirit, or he must rebel" (Keve, 1974, p. 42).

When something so fundamental as human touch is almost entirely absent from a person's life, written communication becomes all the more essential. In this realm, too, there are constant barriers. Even for those who work, prison labor wages are so low that many prisoners have difficulty obtaining stamps, paper and other basic necessities. Censorship of both incoming and outgoing mail is rampant and arbitrary. Even then, because prisoners are usually forbidden from writing to each other or anyone on parole, they are isolated from many of their comrades, sometimes for decades. Phone calls, often costing more than a dollar per minute, are difficult and infrequent for many prisoners, their families and other outside supporters. The situation is even direr for those in solitary confinement or "administrative segregation", "special housing", or "control units", as the most current euphemisms would have it. Political organizing is labeled "gang" or "terrorist" behavior, and many PP/POWs languish in solitary. These labels – "gang member", "terrorist" and "criminal", among others – are part of a system of language that seeks to exert control through classification and repression.

The importance of giving PP/POWs and other prisoners a chance to tell their own stories in their own words has long been recognized. In her introduction to *Imprisoned in America*, Cynthia Owen Philip describes how writing in prison can contribute to self-understanding and emotional health. The results are amplified when such efforts are published: "And so I have taken the role of listener and collector in hopes that, through their communications, prisoners might begin to break down the barriers that so falsely exist between them and those who are not in prison" (Philip, 1973, pp. xiv-xv).

Those voices can in turn have a tremendous impact on the individuals and movements in "free" society. Imprisoned civil rights leaders, including Malcolm X, Huey P. Newton and Bobby Seale, wrote some of their most important works from prison. George Jackson (1970) wrote his pivotal book, *Soledad Brother*, as a series of letters to family, friends and supporters, sparking a passionate movement among prisoners and supporters, and riots when he was killed in 1971.

4STRUGGLEMAG AS A WORK-IN-PROGRESS

4strugglemag editor Jaan Laaman has been an activist since the sixties, when he was involved with groups like the United Steelworkers of America, Students for a Democratic Society (SDS), and other anti-war and anti-imperialist groups. In 1984, he was arrested as one of the Ohio 7, and is serving a total 98-year sentence. From prison, he has contributed to socialist and revolutionary journals, and was involved in the publication of the New England Prisoners Association (NEPA) paper.

From the very first page of the zine, Laaman makes his interest in ongoing dialogue clear: "While 4strugglemag is primarily electronic, hard copies are available for prisoners and others who can't access the Internet. We encourage readers to respond, critique, and carry on the discussions in the magazine". He stresses the dual goals of the project: "I hope 4strugglemag will become a way for at least some PPs to further contribute to the anti-war, social justice and revolutionary struggle. At the same time this will remind readers that PPs do exist and languish in U.S. prisons. It will help raise our profile as we contribute to ongoing struggles".

4strugglemag is published three times a year and it is now in its fifth year of uninterrupted publication. Our subscribers have grown from a few dozen to a few hundred, as prisoners got hold of the magazine, requesting more and more copies. Online, we have more than 15,000 visits a month.

The project has an abolitionist orientation and positions prisoner struggle within a larger anti-imperialist political context. This means that we do not simply focus on "prison issues", but also publish articles on other political issues and world events, and promote the political development of those on the inside and out. Central to this position is the recognition that imprisoned people amount to more than their current status as prisoners. In the case of PPs especially, those of us on the outside have much to learn from their vast political study and years of experience, which should not be devalued by their present circumstances. Their first-hand experience of the lengths the state is willing to go to in order to exert power often leads to much sharper and more valuable analysis than that coming from outside. For us, the prison struggle involves integrating those prisoners' voices in our everyday work around *all* issues, not just those pertaining to prisoners.

CONSCIOUS PRISONERS

Our correspondence with "social prisoners" grows each day, as they learn of our efforts and begin to participate in our dialogue. We send more than 200 printed copies to prisons across Canada and the United States, where each issue is shared among multiple prisoners and used in prisoner-organized study groups.

The majority of our prison readers are those who have become politically conscious while in prison, and the voice of this group has grown significantly in the magazine in recent issues. For example, one such prisoner – Akili Castlin – began a dialogue about the relationship between the older generation of political prisoners and the younger, "hip hop generation", currently being imprisoned at an alarming rate. His first letter, sent to us in the summer of 2006, sparked a discussion that continues to this day, and has included responses from PPs such as Mumia Abu-Jamal and Herman Bell. We are excited to see bridges being built across this generational divide, as each generation has much to learn from the other. For younger prisoners, the older PPs serve as guides through the maze of prison bureaucracy and brutality; as teachers of political theory, history and the struggle of recent decades; and as role models who made real contributions to political struggle. Older PPs can also learn from the energy, insights and enthusiasm of the youth, who can offer salient critiques of how political movements can stay relevant to contemporary circumstances. Most importantly, these articles and letters have begun what we have always wanted to accomplish with 4strugglemag: real dialogue.

CERTAIN DAYS:
FREEDOM FOR POLITICAL PRISONERS CALENDAR
AND OTHER PROJECTS

Two of the outside organizers who work on 4strugglemag have also been fortunate enough to work on the Certain Days: Freedom for Political Prisoners Calendar (see www.certaindays.org) – a collaborative project with political prisoners David Gilbert, Robert Seth Hayes and Herman Bell.

Others, including groups like Jericho and the publishers Kersplebedeb, AG Press, and PM Press, have and continue to print in-depth writings from political prisoners. We hope that all social justice groups will discover the value of including prisoners' voices not just in prison-centric discourses, but in every publication, event, and major discussion.

Communication and action are at the heart of revolutionary movements. Dissent in the realm of the symbolic must be accompanied by daily, active struggle in the realm of the real. Consciousness raising and movement building will come as prisoners develop their own themes, identities and demands. Those who hope to facilitate such work from the outside must increase possibilities and spaces for reflection, and encourage dialogue between prisoners who are kept apart. As Paolo Friere put it: "But to substitute monologue, slogans and communiqués for dialogue is to attempt to liberate the oppressed with the instruments of domestication... To achieve this praxis, however, it is necessary to trust in the oppressed and their ability to reason" (Friere, 1970, p. 53).

REFERENCES

Foucault, Michel (1977) *Discipline and Punish: The Birth of the Prison*, New York: Pantheon.

Friere, Paolo (1970) *Pedagogy of the Oppressed*, Trans. Myra Bergman Ramos. New York: The Seabury Press.

Jackson, George L. (1994[1970]) *Soledad Brother*, Chicago: Lawrence Hill Books.

Keve, Paul W. (1974) *Prison Life and Human Worth*. Minneapolis: University of Minnesota Press.

Laaman, Jaan (ed.) (2004) *4strugglemag: From the Hearts and Minds of North American Political Prisoners and Friends*, 1 (Winter).

Philip, Cynthia O. (ed.) (1973) *Imprisoned in America: Prison Communications 1776 to Attica*, New York: Harper & Row.

CONTACT 4STRUGGLEMAG

4strugglemag
P.O. Box 97048
RPO Roncesvalles Ave.
Toronto, Ontario
M6R 3B3 Canada

Email:
jaanlaaman@gmail.com

BOOK REVIEWS

Exiled Voices: Portals of Discovery
by Susan Nagelsen (ed.)
Henniker: New England College Press (2008), 272 pp.
Reviewed by Gordon Groulx

Set against the backdrop of punitive crime-control policies and mass incarceration, *Exiled Voices* showcases the creative works of thirteen prisoners from across the United States. The objective of this collection of poems, short stories and drama is twofold: 1) it strives to give a voice to the many men and women who have been silenced by virtue of their incarceration; and 2) it serves as a tool of enlightenment and a source of change by providing first-hand accounts of the harrowing realities of imprisonment. While the featured writings are the focal point of this book, they are complemented by an Introduction written by Robert Johnson and an Afterword by Susan Nagelsen, both of which provide telling descriptions of the problem of imprisonment in the United States. Nagelsen also provides a preamble to each writer's work, which, in most cases, includes autobiographical information and a photograph.

The writings in this book are as diverse as the writers themselves. Some pieces focus on childhood experiences of abuse, such as Yvette Louisell's short story, "Size". Others, including a poem by Philip Horner, entitled "Stumpy", speak of the resilience and strength of the human spirit, even under conditions of confinement. The central theme of this collection, however, is the anguish that goes along with a life behind bars. In "Diary of a Lifetime in Blue", Laos Chuman reflects on the reality of sexual assault in prison, whereas William Van Poyck's "Fake Identity" describes, from a very interesting perspective, the suffering, abuse and neglect routinely experienced by mentally-ill prisoners. Also remarkable are works by Charles Huckelbury and Tracy Atkins. In his short story "Riding the Tiger", Huckelbury speaks to the experience of being exposed to pepper gas and conveys what it means to lose a friend to a prison system that begets violence. In her piece "The Funeral", written in a time of immense pain, Atkins refers to her prison sentence as a metaphor for death and reflects on how her experience of incarceration has made her feel forgotten and hollow.

The nature of this collection is such that it is suitable for any reader. The featured pieces are relatively short, yet in no way lack vivid detail or eloquence. The Introduction and Afterword are also straightforward and free of academic jargon, serving only to provide context and closure to the various writings. Although the book contains political overtones, reflecting on the *problem* of the prison from the point of view of those who are incarcerated, the featured works are also creative representations in their own right. This allows the book to be educational for those interested in issues of imprisonment, and also enjoyable for anyone with an open mind and an appreciation for the art of written word.

Exiled Voices exposes the reader to first-hand accounts of prison life and to a different kind of prisoner than is typically portrayed in the media. In doing so, it questions our use of incarceration as a response to crime and challenges many taken-for-granted assumptions about imprisonment. Regardless of how one reads this book, they should see in it a reflection of the many problems associated with the prison. They should also discover behind each piece not a 'criminal', but a fellow human being with a voice, an undeniable gift for writing and a story to tell.

ABOUT THE REVIEWER

Gordon Groulx is currently a doctoral student in Sociology at York University (Canada). His research interests include discourses and practices of imprisonment, as well as the intersection between science, technology and criminal justice. His MA thesis examined the changes to Canada's prison system that were recently proposed in the Ministry of Public Safety's Review Panel Report. His PhD research will explore issues of imprisonment and technology in Canada.

Punishing the Poor:
The Neoliberal Government of Social Insecurity
by Loïc Wacquant
Durham: Duke University Press (2009), 408 pp.
Reviewed by Patrick Derby

The punitive turn in penal policy experienced in the United States is not the result of increased "criminal insecurity" argues Loïc Wacquant in *Punishing the Poor*. Rather, it is a government response to the "social insecurity" accompanying the ascendency of neoliberalism. Wacquant posits that the wave of penalization serves to curtail (urban) disorder, spawned by economic deregulation and the desocialization of wage labour, while at the same time imposing precarious employment upon those at the lower rungs of the class and ethnoracial hierarchy.

Punishing the Poor is organized into four parts, allowing Wacquant to build his argument in a clear and compelling manner, which he does by meticulously detailing American developments in both the realm of welfare and criminal justice at the turn of the new millennium. The first two parts of the monograph – "Poverty of the Social State" and "Grandeur of the "Penal State" – explore the relationship between the rise of precarious and poverty-wage employment, the unraveling of social protections and the criminalization of poverty, and the expansion and extension of the punitive apparatus. The application of disciplinary programs to segments of the population on some form of public assistance (workfare), which serve to push them into the marginal sectors of the employment market conjoins with the extended carceral net (prisonfare), targeted at dispossessed urban districts, to create "a single apparatus for the management of poverty that aims at effecting the authoritarian rectification of the behaviors of population recalcitrant to the emerging economic and symbolic order" (p. 14).

In the third part – "Privileged Targets" – Wacquant turns his attention to two categories that are discriminately ensnared in the carceral net: the unemployed 'street thug' of the black ghetto and the sex offender, especially the roving and unattached pedophile. Wacquant explains that casting these figures to panoptic and penal apparatuses serves the expressive function of reinforcing the demarcation between the 'law-abiding' and the 'criminal'. Those demonstrating characteristics deemed negative by the dominant economic, social and racial order (i.e. poverty, immorality, blackness) are subjected to supervision and regulation, corrective discipline, and/or segregation.

Dissecting the U.S. penal state is not Wacquant's end goal; rather, it is conducted to explore the "invention of neoliberalism in action", in an effort to discover the probable contours of the future penal apparatuses of European and Latin American countries that have embarked on a neoliberal path. The book's final section – "European Declinations" – examines the transposition of American-style governance of social insecurity to contemporary Europe, drawing on the law-and-order developments within France as an empirical referent. Wacquant argues that at the opening of the twenty-first century France is taken by American law-and-order policies, seduced by many of its exported myths. Identifying numerous American penal policies that France has assimilated, Wacquant is also careful to point out that the alignment or convergence of penal policy never entails perfect replication, due to legal, national, cultural differences, among others. In France, the deeper roots of the social state and a weaker hold of individualist ideology has meant the fusion of social and punitive regulation, while the increased penalization of poverty is effected primarily through the police rather than the prison, as in the United States.

Punishing the Poor contributes to socio-legal literatures on the governance of poverty and crime, demonstrating that new insights emerge when brining the developments in welfare and criminal justice policy together under a common analytical frame that is sensitive to both their material and symbolic effects. This book is a must read for academics, students, and activists engaged with, or interested in, the socio-politics of race, poverty, and incarceration.

ABOUT THE REVIEWER

Patrick Derby is a doctoral student in the Department of Sociology at Queen's University (Kingston, Ontario). He is a member of the Surveillance Studies Centre and a founding member of the Surveillance Cameras Awareness Network (SCAN). Patrick's research interests include the political economy of punishment and crime control, as well as the new technologies of surveillance and control. His doctoral dissertation critically explores the politics of automated license plate recognition (ALPR) as an emerging law enforcement technology.

Youth in a Suspect Society: Democracy or Disposability? by Henry A. Giroux
New York: Palgrave Macmillan (2009), 237 pp.
Reviewed by Mike Larsen

Democracy, as a political and cultural framework, must be continuously renewed through participation, reproduced through education, and reinvented through critique. If it is to live up to its promise, it must also be protected from both the authoritarian impulses of states and the reductionist calculations of the market. For Henry A. Giroux, this ongoing project of engagement and struggle hinges on the operation of robust public spheres populated by politically literate and active citizens. It follows that this sort of informed engagement is itself dependent upon practices of critical education, and on sustained social investment in young people, and by extension, in the future. The current state and trajectory of democracy in a given society can therefore be assessed by examining the way it envisions and treats its youth.

Starting from this premise, Giroux, in *Youth in a Suspect Society*, sets out to evaluate the prospects for American democracy at a time when "[y]oung people have become a generation of suspects in a society destroyed by the merging of market fundamentalism, consumerism, and militarism" (p.12). His particular focus in this text is on the intersection of two trends: 1) the relentless commodification of youth culture – and ultimately, of youth themselves – and 2) the operation of a biopolitics[1] of disposability that increasingly exposes youth to the coercive and exclusionary mechanisms of the punishing state. In naming the contemporary socio-cultural context a 'suspect society', Giroux draws attention to the tendency to construct young people – and particularly urban, racialized youth – as pervasive sources of potential danger, destined to be socialized as docile consumers or managed through surveillance and control.

The book begins with a discussion of neoliberalism and the politics of disposability, understood in relation to the plight of youth. Giroux draws on Zygmunt Bauman's (2004) text *Wasted Lives: Modernity and its Outcasts,* which explores the ways in which globalization actively produces – and then manages and disposes of – populations deemed superfluous and excludable. Having set the stage, the book then proceeds in sections to discuss youth and the pedagogy of commodification, education and the youth-crime complex, and youth and academic unfreedom. Giroux concludes by returning to his critique of neoliberalism and expanding on it through a careful engagement with the literature on biopolitics. The conclusion argues for the development of a "[b]iopolitics in the interest of global democracy", defined as "a struggle over those modes of state and corporate sovereignty that control the means of life and death" (p.188). The structure of *Youth in a Suspect Society* means that the core content about youth is bookended by sections that provide political, economic, historical, and theoretical context, which makes for a compelling and grounded though wide-ranging text.

The second chapter, 'Locked Up: Education and the Youth Crime Complex' may be of particular interest to readers of the *JPP*. In the preceding chapter, Giroux discusses the role of neoliberal market sovereignty in the construction of youth as depoliticized individualized consumers. If consumption is on one side of the neoliberal coin, waste is on the other, and the second chapter explores the management of youth deemed to constitute disposable populations. This management is accomplished through a growing "youth control complex"[2] that links institutions sharing a vision of youth as eternally suspicious and potentially threatening. Giroux argues that "[w]hile all youth are now suspect, poor minority youth have become especially targeted by modes of social regulation, crime control, and disposability that have become the major prisms that now define many of the public institutions and spheres that govern their lives" (p.78). The prison is a central institution in this regard, as long-term incapacitation and exclusion has become the preferred 'solution' for all manner of social problems. Drawing on the works of Angela Davis, Jonathan Simon, Loïc Wacquant, and a number of others, Giroux discusses mass incarceration as a phenomenon that has been driven by the imprisonment of young people of colour. He describes ongoing efforts to have youth treated as adults by a criminal justice system that is increasingly unwilling to extend any special consideration to juveniles, and the growth of the specialized youth incarceration sector. He also discusses the increasing adoption of carceral techniques and modalities by public schools concerned with governing youth through crime. The convergence of the school and the prison takes a variety of forms, including the adoption of 'zero tolerance' policies, lowered thresholds for suspension and expulsion, and the incorporation of fences, cameras, security checkpoints, and armed guards into the scholastic setting. While Giroux is by no means the first author to engage with the prizonization of schools and the criminalization of youth, his treatment of these topics here is compelling, accessible, and enhanced by its situation within a broader discussion of neoliberalism and racialized biopolitics.

Youth in a Suspect Society builds upon and extends a line of inquiry that Giroux has been developing in a series of recent books. Readers familiar with these texts will recognize in *Youth in a Suspect Society* the central themes of Giroux' social and cultural theory: neoliberalism as a political, cultural, and economic system and form of public pedagogy that exacerbates structural inequalities and preaches a market fundamentalism while eroding the democratic public sphere (see Giroux 2004); the advance of the neo-authoritarian (in)security state and the militarization of everyday life (Giroux 2005; Giroux 2007); the political mobilization of spectacles of terror, fear, and violence (Giroux 2006a); the racialized biopolitics of disposability in the 21st Century (see Giroux 2006b); and a sustained focus on youth, public education, and critical thought.

One of the highlights of this text is the balance it strikes between being an analysis and blistering critique of the plight of American youth under late modern conditions on the one hand, and a call to arms grounded in a deep commitment to the democratic and emancipatory potential of critical and sustained public education and engagement on the other. The data could easily support a more dystopian tone, but Giroux is careful to focus on possibilities for resistance, substantive citizenship, and push-back. In the future, it would be interesting to read a revised edition of *Youth in a Suspect Society* that broadens the focus beyond the USA to look at geographic and cultural variances in the treatment of youth as bodies defined by commodification or disposability. His current conceptual and theoretical influences would lend themselves well to such a study. In the meantime, though, he offers other researchers, educators, activists and citizens much food for thought, and I look forward to seeing how some of his ideas – particularly the notion of the 'suspect society', his treatment of the youth crime complex, and the call for the development of a biopolitics in the interest of global democracy – are taken up.

ENDNOTES

[1]   In brief, understood as the politics of life itself, concerned with "ordering, regulating, and producing life" (p.169), of controlling bodies and populations, and, at the most negative end of the spectrum, of disallowing life to the point of death.

[2]   This concept emerges from the work of Victor Rios, who describes it as "an ecology of interlinked institutional arrangements that manages and controls the everyday lives of inner-city youth of color" (p.3).

REFERENCES

Bauman, Zygmunt (2004) *Wasted Lives: Modernity and its Outcasts*, Cambridge: Polity.

Giroux, Henry A. (2007) *The University in Chains: Confronting the Military-Industrial-Academic Complex*, Boulder: Paradigm Publishers.

Giroux, Henry A. (2006a) *Beyond the Spectacle of Terrorism: Global Uncertainty and the Challenge of the New Media*, Boulder: Paradigm Publishers.

Giroux, Henry A. (2006b) *Stormy Weather: Katrina and the Politics of Disposability*, Boulder: Paradigm Publishers.

Giroux, Henry A. (2005) *Against the New Authoritarianism: Politics After Abu Ghraib*, Winnipeg: Arbeiter Ring Publishing.

Giroux, Henry A. (2004) *The Terror of Neoliberalism: Authoritarianism and the Eclipse of Democracy*, Aurora: Garamond Press.

ABOUT THE REVIEWER

Mike Larsen is a PhD Candidate in Sociology at York University, and a Researcher at the York Centre for International and Security Studies. He is Co-managing Editor of the *Journal of Prisoners on Prisons*. His work deals with the politics of secrecy and suspicion, with a focus on Canada's security certificate regime and its mechanisms and institutions of detention and control. His most recent article (with Justin Piché) is "Exceptional State, Pragmatic Bureaucracy, and Indefinite Detention: The Case of the Kingston Immigration Holding Centre", published in Volume 24(2) of the *Canadian Journal of Law and Society* (2009). Mike can be reached at mlarsen@yorku.ca.

Anthony Papa is an artist, writer, noted advocate against the war on drugs and co-founder of the Mothers of the New York Disappeared. His opinion pieces about the drug war have appeared in the *Huffington Post*, among others. He is a public speaker and college lecturer on his art and on criminal justice issues. Currently, he is a communications specialist for Drug Policy Alliance in NYC. Papa is the author of *15 to Life: How I Painted My Way to Freedom* (Feral House, 2004), a memoir about his experience of being sentenced to state prison for a first-time, non-violent drug offense under New York's draconian Rockefeller Drug Laws. *The New York Times, The Washington Post, The Nation,* National Public Radio, "Democracy Now", Court TV, "Extra", and C-Span have interviewed him. Papa has appeared on nationally syndicated talk shows such as "Charles Grodin", "Geraldo Rivera", and "Catherine Crier Live". His art has been exhibited at the Whitney Museum of American Art in New York as well as other venues.

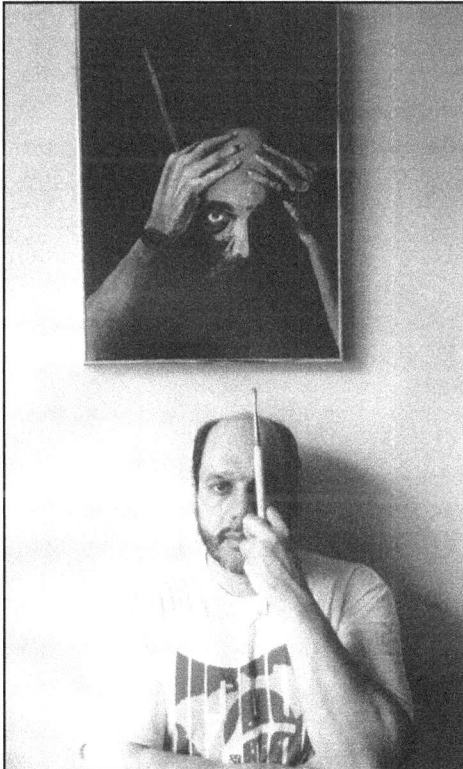

Front Cover: "Fifteen Years to Life" – 1988
Anthony Papa

In 1988, I was sitting in my cell and picked up a mirror. I saw a man who was going to be spending the most productive years of his life locked in a cage. I set up a canvas and captured the image, which I named "15 to Life". In 1994, this self-portrait was exhibited at the Whitney Museum of American Art. *New York Times* art critic Roberta Smith wrote that it was an "ode to art as a mystical, transgressive act that is both frightening and liberating, releasing uncontrollable emotions of all kinds". In 1997, after 12 years in prison, I received executive clemency from Governor George Pataki. Upon release I began having exhibits and used my art as an instrument to speak out against inhumane drug laws.

I use my art as a means of visually translating the deep emotional responses of the human condition. My life choices forced me to discover my hidden artistic talent. In the same way, I try to make that intuitive connection with the viewer of my art by living through my work, breaking down barriers that separate us from truth.

Back Cover: White Butterflies, Blue Hudson – 1995
Anthony Papa

I find symbolic expression of imprisonment in the blades of the many yards of razor wire woven around the sides, tops and bottoms of the many yards of electrified fences, which stand as guards protecting the thirty-foot walls of Sing Sing. I often depict the blades of razor wire against the background of the Hudson River. Each blade represents a double-edged sword, cutting the fabric of life between beauty and ugliness, between the freedom of the Hudson and the pathos of imprisonment, an all-consuming reminder about on which side of life the prisoner lives.

When I picked up a paintbrush, the hand of freedom was my own, and I have been painting my way to freedom ever since, turning barbed wire into butterflies.

Kinnari Jivani was born and raised in India. She is fluent in Gujarati, Hindi and English. She has a B.S. In microbiology from the University of Mumbai. At the age of 20, she was arrested, then sentenced to 11 to 20 years of imprisonment in Michigan. Her earliest release date is in January 2001, after which she faces deportation. Since her incarceration she has been discovering and exploring her talent for painting and writing. Her artwork has been featured in the Michigan Bar Journal and the Artist Magazine. Her paintings have been shown in the Annual Exhibition of Art by Michigan Prisoners for many years and has consistently won first place awards. Her writings have been published in *The Change Agent,* a magazine for social change; *A Crack in the Concrete,* an anthology of poems*; Bhumika,* a feminist magazine; *The Project V-Day: Until the Violence Stops,* headed by Eve Ensler; and in the *Michigan Review of Prisoner Creative Writing*, an anthology. She is a yoga instructor and volunteers weekly yogasana classes in the facility. She is now housed in the Women's Huron Valley Correctional Facility in Michigan.

Back Cover: A Tribute to 26/11 – 2009
Kinnari Jivani

On November 2008, when Mumbai came under terrorist attack the world's TV screens filled with images of burning Taj Hotel, bullet-marked and blood-covered railway station, residential buildings, café, hospital, and devastated people of Mumbai. Like most of the world, I was overwhelmed to see the city of my birth under attack, and I was concerned for my family's safety. As a young girl I'd played on the cobble-stones of the Gateway of India and gazed at the magnificent Taj Hotel; seeing it on fire with people trapped inside affected me deeply. Thousands of miles away from home, incarcerated in Michigan, I couldn't do anything. I cried and prayed, prayed and cried. Eventually, I learned that my family was safe but nonetheless many lives were lost.

I couldn't participate in the candle-light vigil, so I painted my emotions and created "A Tribute to 26/11". It is my tribute to Mumbai and the people who collected the broken pieces and have stood up once again with brilliant resilience. When the Gateway of India was built by the British, India, Pakistan and Bangladesh were all one country; we fought shoulder to shoulder for freedom from the British. But in 1947 when the British left behind their legacy of "divide and conquer", we split apart for land, religion, and name. Although we are still at war, I believe that most common folk in India and Pakistan really care for each other; it is politicians of extremists who love to continue the spread of hatred.

The woman in the painting is wearing a t-short with the flag of India and the quote "United we stand undivided. If we as common folk of India and Pakistan keep out ancient bond of kinship alive perhaps we can overcome the hatred. My tribute is to these local courageous people who suffer the most but carry the beautiful light in their daily lives.

The woman could be me or any young woman in Mumbai. I am a student of yoga and I have mastered the head stand posture. I learned that to get into this posture it takes more than physical balance and have linked it to the concept of resilience. The book her head lies on is also titled resilience and the blue ball could be a glass globe – to express the fragileness of our existence- could be a ball I played with as a young girl, could be of a glass marble with which so many children in India play. Sometimes the objects or symbols in my work represent more than one thing because life is complex like that!

JPP articles often draw on a wide range of reference material, including academic texts, journal articles, newspaper and magazine articles, online publications, legislation, case law, and works of fiction. We strive to publish detailed bibliographical information using a standardized format, in order to facilitate cross-referencing. Contributors are encouraged to use the following referencing format for their article submissions. We recognize that it is sometimes difficult or impossible for our contributors to provide full reference information, and we will always take the time to complete partial references.

FORMAT GUIDELINES AND EXAMPLES

In-text Citation – Single Reference

(Author Last Name, date, p. x)

Example:
In prison, as in other 'social' institutions, the focus of education is often the promotion of "social utility and conformity" (Hassine, 1997, p. 37).

In-text Citation – Multiple References

(Author(s) 1 Last Name(s), date; Author(s) 2 Last Name(s), date)

Example:
It also proposes new and less costly strategies that are more humane and effective (Richards and Ross, 2001; Ross and Richards 2002, 2003; Jones 2003; Newbold, 2003; Terry, 2003a, 2003b).

Book

Author Last Name, Author First Name (date) *Title of Book*, City of Publication: Publisher.

Example:
Christie, Nils (1999) *Crime Control As Industry*, London: Routledge.

Edited Volume (Reference to the Volume)

Editor Last Name, Editor First Name (ed.) (date) *Title of Book*, City of Publication: Publisher.

Example, single editor:
Gaucher, Bob (ed.) (2002) *Writing As Resistance: The Journal of Prisoners on Prisons Anthology (1988-2002)*, Toronto: Canadian Scholars Press Inc.

Example, multiple editors (note that only the first editor is listed with last name first):
Mauer, Marc and Meda Chesney-Lind (eds.) (2002) *Invisible Punishment: The Collateral Consequences of Mass Imprisonment*, New York: The New Press.

Chapter in an Edited Volume

Chapter Author Last Name, Chapter Author First Name (date) "Chapter Title", in Editor First Name Initial, Editor Last Name(ed.), *Edited Volume Title*, City of Publication: Publisher, pp. x-y.

Example (with multiple editors):
Richie, Beth E. (2004) "Challenges Incarcerated Women Face as they Return to their Communities: Findings from Life Histories Interviews", in M. Chesney-Lind & L. Pasko (eds.), *Girls, Women and Crime: Selected Readings*, Thousand Oakes: Sage Publications, pp. 231-245.

Article in an Academic Periodical

Author Last Name, Author First Name (date) "Article Title", *Journal Title*, Volume(Number): x-y.

Example:
Huckelbury, Charles (2006) "Made in the U.S.A.: A Postmodern Critique", *Journal of Prisoners on Prisons*, 15(1): 4-16.

Newspaper or Magazine Article (Print)

Author Last Name, Author First Name (date) "Article Title", *Periodical Title*, p. x-y – Month day.

Example:
Beplate, Justin (2005) "Express or Exploit", *Times Literary Supplement*, pp. 13-14 – December 23.

Newspaper or Magazine Article (Online)

Author Last Name, Author First Name (date) "Article Title", *Publication Title* – Month day, retrieved from URL.

Example:
Evans, Jon (2008) "Big Brother is Watching Them. OK?", *The Walrus* December 8, retrieved from http://www.walrusmagazine.com/ blogs/2008/12/08/big-brother-is-watching-them/.

Online Article (General)

Author Last Name, Author First Name [or, if author details unavailable, Website Proprietor] (date) "Article Title", *Website Name* – Month day, retrieved from URL.

Example:
CBC News (2008) "Prison Ombudsman May Release Report into Ashley Smith's Death", cbc.ca – October 27, retrieved from http://www.cbc.ca/ canada/new-brunswick/story/2008/10/27/nb-smith-ombudsman.html).

Legal Jurisprudence

Standards of legal citation vary according to jurisdiction and legal system. Given the international scope of the JPP, it would be impractical for us to insist on a single referencing format for jurisprudence. We encourage authors to adopt a style that is consistent and appropriate to their location. For Canadian references, and as a general guideline, we recommend the

Canadian Guide to Uniform Legal Citation, a.k.a. the "McGill Guide," which uses the following format:

Style of cause, [date] [if not indicated by a neutral citation], neutral citation [if available], law report volume number, law report series, page number, court [if applicable].

Examples:

Hopp v. Lepp, [1980] 2S.C.R. 192.

Suresh v. Canada (Minister of Citizenship and Immigration), 1 S.C.R.3 ([2002)] 1 S.C.R. 3.

Legislation

Legislative Assembly Name (date) *Act Name, Bill Name*.X

Example:

Parliament of Canada (2001) *Immigration and Refugee Protection Act, S.C. 2001, c-27.*

Report

Author Last Name, Author First Name [or, if author details unavailable, Agency Name] (date) "Sub-chapter Title", [and / or] *Report Title –* Month day, City of Publication: Publisher.

Example:

Office of the Auditor General of Canada (2008) "Chapter 7: Detention and Removal of Individuals - Canada Border Services Agency", *Report of the Auditor General of Canada to the House of Commons –* May, Ottawa: Minister of Public Works and Government Services Canada.

Institutional Policy Document or Communication

Institution Name (date) *Document Title –* Month day.

Example:

Canada Border Services Agency (2006) *KIHC President's Directive PD 566-4: Detainee Counts –* March.